I MIGHT HAVE TOLD YOU THIS BEFORE.

50 years. 50 stories.
50 observations.

By Jay Martin

NAUTILUS PUBLISHING
Oxford, Mississippi

Editor's note.

All the photos in this book come from one wall in Jay Martin's home. You might say, it's a wall as wide, as tall, and as full as the life it marks – but a wall isn't big enough for that.

For bulk orders, contact:
Boys and Girls Clubs of Greater Memphis at www.bgcm.org

This book can be obtained only through a donation to the Boys and Girls Clubs of Greater Memphis. Details are available on the website.

Nautilus Publishing Company
426 South Lamar Blvd, Suite 16, Oxford, Mississippi 38673
Tel: 1-866-811-9680 • 662-513-0159 • Fax: 662-234-9266
www.nautiluspublishing.com • info@nautiluspublishing.com

Martin, Jay (1943-   )
        I Might Have Told You This Before — 1st ed.

        Cover design by Chung Design

Printed in Canada

10   9   8   7   6   5   4   3   2   1

Acknowledgments

To "My People."

This book is dedicated to the more than 50,000 members of the Juice Plus+® family whose tireless efforts to Inspire Healthy Living Around The World are making a difference in the lives of millions.

My thanks.

First, I would like to thank my mother and father for the endless words of wit and wisdom they shared with me over the years.

Secondly, I would like to thank my wife, Sandra, and our children Meredith, Jay, Melanie and Greg, and our grandchildren Whitney, Taylor, Patrick, Maisie and Dylan, who provide inspiration for me every day.

Thirdly, to my friend and editor, Dan Conaway, who helped me bring these stories from the stage to the page without missing a beat, a heartfelt thanks.

Last – thank you again, "My People," for all the laughs and love that kept me going all these years.

This book is priceless. But for a donation, I'll let you borrow it forever.

In the last 50 years, I have spoken to over a million people in 23 countries. I have never charged a fee nor sold a book or tape. I don't intend to start now.

This book cannot be bought, but it can be had.

It can be obtained only through a donation to the Boys and Girls Clubs of Greater Memphis. Our clubs are not only changing the lives of the kids we serve but are also creating a model for other clubs around the country, offering a brighter light in the dark and a brighter day tomorrow.

Just because you have this book, they'll have a better chance.

Thank you for your donation. Find out more about what we're doing and the part you're playing at www.bgcm.org

Please note.

No one can write a book without borrowing something from somebody sometime.

For me it was from my hero, my father, and my heroes, Will Rogers and Mark Twain, speakers and authors like Lewis Grizzard, Worthington Hipple, Judge Ziglar and Robert Townsend and the occasional preacher, politician, house painter, coach and the guy on the third stool down.

I must confess however that almost all of this came from my own real life experiences. This is me off the stage and on the page. Enjoy. I hope.

If anyone is offended, or even disappointed, by my writings please tear out the offending pages and send them along with a self-addressed stamped envelope for a full pro rata refund of (9 cents per page) less a small handling charge.

Feel free to include your comments. However, if I find them offensive, there will be a large handling charge, and you might be offended by what I put in that envelope.

Introduction

"You can't make them buy if you can't make them laugh."

On my desk is a coffee cup I picked up in Boston at the Kennedy library. On it is a quote from JFK. "There are three things which are real: God, Human Folly and Laughter. The first two are beyond our comprehension so we must do what we can with the third."

In writing this book, I did the best I could with the third, and was guided by the one principle of storytelling that I've always tried to adhere to – "Don't let the truth get in the way of a good yarn."

I won't.

In his wonderful short story called The Mesmerizer, Mark Twain tells of a hypnotist who once came to Hannibal and performed nightly in a tent. His star subject was a local by the name of Wallace. It seems that Wallace could be put "under" in a matter of minutes every night. The effectiveness of the first few performances were also enhanced by the fact that Wallace had the reputation of never telling a lie. As you might imagine, by a little later in the week the show grew a bit dull. Twain remembered that the Mesmerizer began to look upon him as a potential replacement subject, "having a sixth sense about the fact that I was not born with Wallace's encumbrance."

Neither was I.

I can summarize my philosophy by relating a story from my neighbor and high school buddy, Spado Speas. Spado is a former president of the American College of Trial Lawyers. He got his nickname from his uncle Spado, a house painter who was married seven times for a total of six weeks, but, as they say, that's another story.

"Spado II" was involved in a lawsuit and was preparing one of his key witnesses for trial. This particular witness was extremely eager to tell his side of the story, and his exuberance caused him to be a little loose with the facts. During the prepping session, Spado was continually having to remind the guy to "stick with what you actually saw and heard; don't throw in what you THINK you know." After about an hour and a dozen or so admonishments, the witness got a little perturbed. "Dammit, Speas," he spit, "I'm going to tell the truth even if I have to lie about it."

So am I.

As to the truth about stories, here's the truth: Lying on paper ain't easy.

As to the value of stories, and if I leave you with nothing else, I'll leave you with this:

You can't make them buy if you can't make them laugh.

Season's Best
TO YOU AND YOURS

AVRIL AND THE GANG

He's fit and fleet of foot

■ After heart procedure, John Di Carlo returned to his old love: running.

► Personal stories A7-8
► How exercise helps A9

By GARY R. BLOCKUS
Of The Morning Call

Di CARLO

◄ Continued From F...

While weeding ...
garden in 1994, he ...
his chest.

"I didn't know ...
like from drinki...
barn] or wanting ...
recalled Di Car...
speaks with an ...

Di Carlo w...
ley Hospital ...
cated a majo...
his arteries ...
plasty, the...
later.

His blo...

As an 18-year-old in the
army stationed in Rome in the
1960s, John Di Carlo found himself
on the receiving end of an angry
captain.

"Something happened and the
captain punished me," said Di Carlo, now 54 and living in Sch-
necksville.

He said, "You have ...
four rounds of the ...
mile,' but ...
lised run ...
another fo ...
four, and ti ...
crazy."

... utes) ...
... miles ...
... before," ...
... g the ...
... sville ...
... pment. ...
... thing, I ...

marathon ...
three times a week an...
25 total miles, practically all on
neighborhood runs. He built up
his mileage gradually, first by
walking, then walking and running, and then marathoning.

Now that would really drive ...

Local stud... promot...

HAIR PIECES
HAIR COLORING
MANICURE

...ar
and Razor
HAIRSTYLING
...NS ROAD
...0462

WOMEN

6 EXPERT STYLISTS
BOOTBLACK

Humor me ...

1. Laugh at yourself publicly and privately, and beware of anyone who can cry on cue.

2. Don't intimidate your management team. If laughing at you and your mistakes is good for you, it will be even better for them.

3. Socialize with your management team. If you want to ruin a good company party, invite as many outsiders as you can.

4. If you plan to work with someone who doesn't have a sense of humor – don't.

5. Getting there isn't half the fun, it's all of it.

Falcons Don't Fly

"The other night I saw you comin' and pulled off the road cause I thought you were spraying for mosquitoes."

The first car I ever owned was a 1960 Ford Falcon, which I purchased used for $400. When I say used I mean used like a rented mule.

Nevertheless, I was a proud owner and decided to adorn it with company signs on both doors and the trunk. I was selling pots and pans at the time and actually tried unsuccessfully to emulate one of my fellow salesmen and make a hood ornament out of a one-quart sauce pan.

I was a cracker jack salesman but never could seem to build an organization. One day I got up the nerve to ask my regional manager why.

"I know exactly why, son. It may hurt your feelings, but since you asked, I'm going to tell you anyway. It's that Falcon pure and simple."

"You mean my car?" I replied.

"I'm glad you didn't call it an automobile."

"What's wrong with it?" I asked.

"How many miles does it have on it?"

"126,000 but you can't see but 26."

"You can hear the other hundred and you'd be surprised what you can see. The other night I saw you comin' and pulled off the road 'cause I thought you were spraying for mosquitoes. I know you're tight, but if you ain't goin' to trade it, do us all a favor and take the company signs off of it."

Well, I decided to trade. I looked around and started lusting after a 1969 Pontiac SJ. I washed and waxed the Falcon, but the old bird had other problems. My car was afflicted with a rare disease that could well prove fatal to my trade-in value.

You could pull in the driveway, turn the switch off, remove the key, put it in your pocket, get out of the car, walk to the front door, check the mail, go get a beer, come back, and the damn thing would still be chugging. Blub…blub...blub…blub…blub.

I didn't think this phenomenon would improve my negotiating position, so I developed a strategy to hide that feature from the salesman. The Pontiac dealership was located at the bottom of a very long hill. My idea was to attain top speed (about 60 mph) coming down the hill, cut the motor off about a mile away, and coast into the dealership after the blub, blub, blubbing stopped.

I made a couple of dry runs and then went for it. Everything went like clockwork. My confidence had never been higher. The old Falcon had never looked better and coughed out its last blub just as the front tires touched the curb of the dealership parking lot.

The salesman came out, let me test drive the Pontiac and ushered me into his cubicle. After going over the options, the warranty, and especially the terms, he shoved about two dozen tiny-type-stuffed pages across the desk for me to sign.

At that point, I went all in and confidently exposed my hole card. "Whatcha goin' give for mine?" I asked sternly, trying to hide the slight squeak in my voice.

He looked at me like I was the class dunce, puffed the last one-half inch of a rancid cigar and said, "Well, bubba, why don't we pull her around on the scales and see what she weighs?"

Too Early To Judge

"Our door opened as far as the chain lock would allow, and a hand that we knew to be Spado's wiggled through and jiggled the keys to the entire Town of Boonville police car fleet."

Every year after baseball season, Coach Simmons, who was also the town's entire police department, would take some players to Cincinnati to see a couple of major league baseball games.

This particular year it was my turn along with two of my best friends, Haggis Brown and Spado Speas. Spado was still in high school, and Haggis and I were on our way to college.

Since the only car Coach Simmons had at his disposal was the Town of Boonville police car, that was our ride – complete with screaming siren, bright blue light, and I-am-the-man signage. Really.

The trip would take about 12 hours so we left around dark planning to arrive in time to check into our hotel, get a nap, and head to the game the next night. The route was through the mountains of West Virginia and then down the Ohio River to Cincinnati.

A couple of hours or so after we left, Coach asked us if we'd like a beer. Really.

Though inexperienced in such matters, we all answered "sure" more in unison than the Pips behind Gladys Knight. The beer he was speaking of was in his trunk – in his trunk in August and not in a cooler – so a hot tall Schlitz it was. And another hot tall Schlitz it was. As the late great George Jones sang, "just one more, and then another."

By the time we reached West Virginia, we would soon be aware that our limit of hot tall Schlitz's – that would be three – had been reached. In West Virginia, they have curves so tight you can see the rear end of your own car. After a series of those, the Pips all got sick in unison. Luckily for us, and the backseat of the Town of Boonville police fleet, Coach Simmons found a place to pull over. While the Pips sent a hot tall Schlitz lava flow down a West Virginia mountainside, promising in unison to spend our lives as missionaries if we could be allowed to live through this night, we were suddenly illuminated in bright light. In this case, the providential light was coming from the headlights of a local West Virginia police officer happening by the hot tall mess. Simmons – no longer to be called Coach – had not partaken of the hot tall Schlitz's, so no crime was committed, and his insistence that the cop "confiscate" the remaining beer was warmly received, again in unison, by the Pips.

Once in Cincinnati, we slept it off, dreaming of our future as missionaries. That night we headed to Crosley Field and became pretty religious about some ice cold Hudepohls. While we returned to the hotel raring to go, Simmons wasn't raring and told us to go to bed, so off to our rooms we went. But not to bed.

Spado, being the youngest, had drawn the short straw and was rooming with Simmons. About an hour passed when there was a knock. Our door opened as far as the chain lock would allow, and a hand that we knew to be Spado's wiggled through and jiggled the keys to the entire Town of Boonville police car fleet. Really.

The rest is a little foggy, and if it ever clears up I may not share it anyway. I have a family. Spado and Haggis are respected citizens.

We headed to Newport, Kentucky, the most "open" town in ten states, and made sure we did the whole tour. We didn't actually stop anybody, but did use both the siren and the blue light on several occasions, causing several pairs of pants to be changed. We arrived back at the hotel safely, but only Haggis recognized that to be a miracle and renewed his vows.

He did become a missionary of sorts, saving the youth of Boonville as the principal of the Town of Boonville school and later chairman of the county school board. Spado Speas became the president of the American College of Trial Lawyers. Coach Simmons had an entire baseball complex named in his honor. Me? I lived at least long enough to tell this story.

Three morals:

Don't drink hot beer. Facebook and Twitter should be outlawed. And what's thrown up on a mountain in West Virginia or flashed in Kentucky should stay there.

Really.

Marbled Easter

"His problem wasn't that I had the marbles, but that I had them in church and that church is where – as it were – I spectacularly lost my marbles."

Last Sunday was Easter. I went to church. We sang "He Arose" and "At the Cross," and I jarred down on the bass well enough for the lady in front of me to suggest that I come to choir practice on Tuesday night. High praise for low talent. After the real choir performed a special program we all settled in for the sermon. I listened to most of what the preacher had to say except for a rather lengthy segment when my mind wandered back to an Easter Sunday service a million stories ago in my hometown of Boonville.

I was in the 5th grade, sitting next to my best friend, Haggis Brown, and his mother, my favorite teacher. I came to church that warm spring morning sporting a brand new blue and white seersucker jacket with trousers to match. I also brought along about 30 or so marbles – including at least ten prize "cat-eyes," six class-A "breadwagons," and three "steelies" about the size of a small golf ball – all loaded in my jacket pockets.

To my knowledge, no church in our area had air conditioning back then. Fans with funeral home advertisements were standard equipment in most sanctuaries, and Boonville Baptist was no exception, with the congregation putting them to good use rather than resting in peace. Early on in the service and hot, I removed my jacket and wadded it up on the pew between Haggis and me.

During the benediction when every head was bowed and every eye was closed, except the one eye of my father, which was always focused on me from his seat in the choir, I tried to discretely pick up my coat and put it on in order to get a head start out the door when the service was finally over. When I caught my father's eye I lost my concentration, my jacket turned upside down, and 30 marbles, including those "breadwagons" and "steelies," hit the hardwood floor in rapid succession, sounding like marble machine gun fire, echoing like a Grand Canyon yodel. You can imagine how embarrassed I was. You can also imagine how sympathetic and understanding Haggis and the rest of my friends were for me – as in not – as in laughing and hooting so hard as to produce snot on Easter jackets as I scrambled frantically to recover my rolling, ricocheting barrage.

However, they were the least of my problems.

On the way home, I got a dose of medieval Catholicism. My father conducted an inquisition that Pope Gregory himself would have gotten exorcised over. In less than one mile, he was able to extract from me that I had won exactly 19 of my marbles playing for "keeps," and that the majority of those had come from Slick Stone, while a few may have come from Junior Williard by way of Raeford Evans. I even confessed that the provenance of the other 11 might be a little iffy.

Somewhere between the one stoplight in our town and my home, the Reformation occurred, and we were back on Protestant ground.

My father, being more of an Old Testament man, felt that a little wrath of God in the woodshed would be in order, but he didn't see any reason to give the marbles back. His problem wasn't that I had the marbles, but that I had them in church and that church is where – as it were – I spectacularly lost my marbles. On Easter. In front of God and everybody.

My mother, more in tune with the teachings of the Apostle Paul and the New Testament, suggested that I could avoid the woodshed by apologizing to everyone involved and returning the marbles. Her favorite expression was "forgiveness lasts forever."

Father for consequences. Mother for forgiveness. After a family discussion – without me present – "we" reached a compromise.

My father and I would visit the woodshed, and I would give the marbles back with the appropriate apologies. I guess the forgiveness lasted forever, but the effects of the woodshed lasted plenty long enough.

I guess you could say they threw the book at me. Both testaments.

Was It Liquor?

*"I thought about lighting up a cigarette and popping a beer to
see if I could change the subject, but decided against it."*

My best friend in college and I had a lot in common. We
played and loved sports; we came from small towns in
moonshine country. Our parents were strict, especially
our fathers. We liked to sing harmony after several beers – not
successfully – chase girls after a few more beers – even less
successfully – and were somehow driven to get into and stay in
trouble – very successfully.

Once in a blue moon we went home on a weekend.

We'd grown up only a few miles apart and usually rode
together. On this particular occasion, I was serving some type of
probationary sentence and was without a car, so we took his. He
was in a more grave situation.

A couple of weeks before he had been caught, after those
several beers, urinating in the front seat of a fellow student's
convertible. I know this sounds terrible, but if you'd known this
particular fellow, you would have peed in his car, too, or at least
cheered while somebody else did. It was that kind of cheering
that attracted "Deputy Dog," chief of our campus police.

My good buddy was in mortal fear that his parents had found
out about his most recent transgression. After dropping me off,
he continued home with a forlorn look on his face and a sincere
"good luck" from me.

The next day he picked me up – still alive, so far, so good – and we started back to school. After all of a hundred yards, I couldn't wait any longer so I asked, "What happened?"

"Not good," was his reply. "They got a letter."

"What'd it say?"

"They might as well have sent pictures."

"What'd your parents say?"

"Same ole crap. They tried to divide and conquer. My old man got me out in the yard and threatened to whip my ass until I was unrecognizable and drive my car into the river with me in it. I'd only seen him this mad five or six times before. Seven, tops."

"What'd you do?"

"I thought about lighting up a cigarette and popping a beer to see if I could change the subject, but decided against it."

"How about your mother?"

"Guilt trip. She said my dad's blood pressure was the highest it had ever been, and he almost had a stroke when he read the letter."

"Did she know the details?"

"No, she said he was ashamed to read it to her, and she hadn't seen him that upset since last summer when he had to make my bail."

"Anything else?"

"Yeah. She said she'd like to ask me a question. 'Son,' she said, 'was it liquor? I've told you more than once that liquor will make you do things you ought not to do.'"

We drove in silence for a quarter mile or so and my buddy reached under his seat and retrieved a pint of Howard Bolin's finest ten-day-old white lightning.

"Let's go do something we ought not to do," he suggested.

"Good idea," was my reply.

A couple of weeks later it was my parents' turn to receive a letter – a letter inviting me to continue my education somewhere else, pretty much anywhere else.

Yes, it was liquor. It makes you pee on yourself and pretty much everybody else.

Holey Haggis

"I'll take slow, lazy and fox smart over fast,
energetic and rock dumb any day."

Haggis Brown was my best friend in school and we're still friends today. His mother was my favorite teacher, and we played football, basketball and baseball on the same team from the fourth grade on. Today we try to play golf. He was one of the slowest and laziest teammates I ever had. He was also the smartest. And that's what got him on all those teams.

One day we were playing baseball archrival Yadkinville (pronounced Yag-en-vil), and were ahead in the bottom of the ninth by a score of 5-3. Yadkinville had runners on first and second with two outs when star player Ugly Hutchins lumbered to the plate. Ugly was a good example of why some people's real first names just don't fit. His should have been Big and Ugly.

Ugly turned on my fastball and jerked it over the first basemen's head into the right field corner with the ugly look and sound of extra bases. Pitchers know that sound. Haggis, with the urgency of an afternoon nap, jogs over to play the carom while Ugly and his teammates circled the bases. "Hurry, Haggis, Hurry," we all yelled – like telling Refrigerator Perry to try the salad.

Finally, Haggis arrived at the fence about the time Ugly was being waved in with the winning run by his third-base coach. As Ugly approached home with the game's final amen, Haggis dropped to his knees by the fence as if to pray. Then he called for an umpire. It seems as if the ball had "found" its way under the fence. Under the rules of baseball, that's a ground rule double. Ugly must return to second base and, more importantly, the guy that was on first – who was already taking his uniform off and grinning at his girlfriend – must go back to third. Result: the next batter hit a grounder to second and we won.

MVP Haggis Brown – play of the day – stuffing an inside the park home run through a hole in the fence and turning it into a double.

I'll take slow, lazy and fox smart over fast, energetic and rock dumb any day.

And I'll continue to make sure I watch every move Haggis makes when he's looking for a ball in the rough.

Experience counts, too.

!LOST!

Black & White
Maincoon Ca
of Java C
king lot o
4/99 at 1:00
lease call th
rtin's at 753-
$REWAR

30th Anniversary
Leadership Conference
Fall 2000

GENERAL RON WATKINS

TENNESSEE

39
CLUB

Qualifiers
Club

12
CLUB

Triple Crown

Qualifiers
Club IV

STAFF

RagApple Lassie
VINEYARDS

FRANK & LENNA HOBSON
Owners

3820 Rockford Rd.   336-367-5252
Boonville, NC 27011   E-mail: Hobcats@aol.com

Milton Wiggins'
"WORLD FAMOUS"
Buntyn
Restaurant
MEMPHIS, TENN.

OPEN
MON. - FRI.
11:00 A.M. - 8:00 P.M

3070
Southern
6 Blocks West of
Memphis State
458-8776

Drink...(while you can "stand")
A 100 year super picture contest
A 1000 year time capsule

For details, directions, parking arrangements,
accomodations, transportation home, legal advice,
physical, mental or spiritual counseling.
Call 753-2190...ask for Sir Isaac Newton.

R.s.v.p. by December 15th   Dress - yes or no

Before gravity takes us hostage, before we completely
forget all our names, and before we start taking mass
quantities of female hormones to ease the aging process.
LET'S PARTY!!
Y'all are invited to the joint 50th Birthday B
celebrating our same year, same month, same day
same hour ??? birthday.

(Just think of us as two 25-year-olds!) Just k
For Sandra Martin and Chris Blair
Friday, June 28, 1996   7 p.m
2931 Johnson Road, Germantown, Tenn
Barbecue dinner by Chef "Hopper" p
"live" band. 50's dress optional. You a
like or nothing at all if you don't comply, but we
let you in anyway. Dress casually. No
Regrets only - "Martins" - 753-2

POSTDATED   5-1-98

$ 1,500
00

AND ANOTHER THING – IN FACT – 50

Word count doesn't count ...

6.   All new forms, brochures, pamphlets, manuals must always sound the death knell of at least two others.

7.   Organizational charts are good only for appeasing people who think they are somehow necessary. People are not rectangles.

8.   Employment contracts – never had one, never read one, never seen one.

9.   Employee Manuals – never read one, never want to see one.

10. Job descriptions – never had one, never read one. Had I, I would have called "bullshit." Every company needs a bullshit meter, and someone would have to call "bullshit" when it goes off. In fact, everyone should yell bullshit" when it goes off.

Find A Buddy

"Show me a Mormon missionary on a bicycle by himself and I'll bet that either he or his partner is lost."

When I visit cities and towns across the globe and speak to audiences both large and small, invariably I'm asked, "If you could give me one piece of advice, what would it be?"

My answer is always the same, "Find a buddy."

When I observe people who are successful, and others trying to be successful, and still others who are waiting to see if they're going to be successful, I see one thing over and over that separates them.

The successful ones have found a partner, a person who shares the same goals and aspirations, someone beside them who's up front with them and has their back.

They've found a buddy.

When I have a chance, I amplify my point.

"A good preacher needs a good Amener." "A full moon shines nine times brighter than a half moon." "The power of two to influence a third is significantly greater than the power of one to influence a second."

Okay, that last one was a bit deep.

Roger Bannister ran the first sub four-minute mile in 1954 all by himself. Almost immediately others began to do it in races with others, but it was years after before someone else ran under four minutes alone.

It even spills over onto religious ground. After all, there's a 2,000-year-old principle called "going out in pairs" that works. Show me a Mormon missionary on a bicycle by himself, and I'll bet that either he or his partner is lost.

Having a partner can keep us out of trouble.

A friend of mine used to work for a boat rental company up on the Tennessee River. Occasionally he would take clients out himself. His boss was a tobacco-chewing, bib-overall-wearing, certified fresh-water redneck they called Tadpole. One day he gave my friend some advice. "Son," he said, "When you take a Baptist out you always need to take another Baptist with him." "Why?" asked my friend. "Cause one by himself will drink all your beer."

If you are excited about what you are doing find someone just as excited. If you are obsessed, find someone that's obsessed as well – or, like what we used to say in western North Carolina, "abscessed", find somebody else that's just that kind of sick. Then you can "infect" others and start an epidemic, maybe even a pandemic, and get all come over with success.

Find A Buddy.

You Can't Do The Job Alone

"Due to my shock at being jerked off the ground so swiftly, I lost my presence of mind and forgot to let go of the rope. Between the second and third floors I met the barrel coming down."

Here's a letter from a friend of mine who works in the claims department of a workers compensation insurance company. He thought I might enjoy it. I did.

Dear Sir:

I am writing in response to your request for more information concerning block #11 on the insurance form which asks for 'cause of injuries' wherein I put 'Trying to do this job alone.' You said you needed more information so I trust the following will be sufficient.

I am a bricklayer by trade, and on the date of the injuries I was laying brick around the top of a four-story building, when I realized I had 500 pounds of brick left over. Rather than carry the bricks down by hand, I decided to put them into a barrel and lower them by a pulley which was fastened to the top of the building. I secured the end of the rope at ground level and went up to the top of the building and loaded the bricks into the barrel and swung it out with the bricks in it. I then went down and untied the rope, holding it securely to insure the slow descent of the barrel.

As you will note in Block #6 of the insurance form, I

weigh 145 lbs.

Due to my shock at being jerked off the ground so swiftly, I lost my presence of mind and forgot to let go of the rope. Between the second and third floors I met the barrel coming down. This accounts for the bruises and lacerations on my upper body.

Regaining my presence of mind, I held tightly to the rope and proceeded up the side of the building not stopping until my right hand jammed in the pulley.

This accounts for my broken thumb.

Despite the pain, I regained my presence of mind and held tightly to the rope. At approximately the same time, however, the barrel of bricks hit the ground and the bottom fell out of the barrel. Devoid of the weight of the bricks, the barrel now weighed about 50 lbs.

I again refer to Block #6 and my weight of 145 lbs.

As you can guess, I began a rapid descent. In the vicinity of the second floor I met the barrel coming back up. This explains the injuries to my legs and lower body.

Slowed only slightly, I continued my descent landing on the pile of bricks. This accounts for my sprained back and internal injuries.

I am sorry to report, however, that at this point, I again lost my presence of mind and let go of the rope, and as you can imagine, the empty barrel crashed down on me.

This accounts for my head injuries.

I trust this answers your concern. Please know that I am finished TRYING TO DO THIS JOB ALONE.

Saying You're Sorry Ain't Enough

"Those of us who would rather not be men shouldn't come to practice on Monday, and those of us who do show up don't need to be late."

Various quotes and stories about Harry Truman illustrate his belief that you can accomplish just about anything as long as you give enough credit to other people and save enough blame for yourself. My father would add that, while taking blame was admirable, it's not always enough. "Saying you're sorry gets old after a while unless you can offer a solution," was his motto.

Yes Sir.

I played for some pretty intense coaches. My high school football coach knocked a referee out during my very first game in uniform. Flat out. My college basketball coach at Wake Forest was forced by the Atlantic Coast Conference to wear a seat belt on the bench for an entire season. Had to be strapped down.

Yes Sir.

But my son's basketball coach may still win the prize. Coach Jerry Peters of Memphis University School won 1,000 basketball games, a distinction only a handful of coaches can claim in the long history of the sport.

Intensity was obviously one of the weapons in coach Peters' arsenal. There are a thousand stories to go with his thousand wins, but I believe the one about his very first game says it all.

When Coach Peters first came to MUS, he coached track and junior high football. The football team he inherited had been winless the previous year. The word was that pre-season practice was like Paris Island, and he intended to stop the losing streak the very first game. He almost did. They lost to a team 13-7 that had beaten them 49-0 the previous year.

The kids were excited about their performance and were looking forward to the rest of the season with optimism. Coach Peters didn't exactly see it that way. Those present said he "laid a cussin' on us that George Carlin would've been embarrassed to hear." He concluded by saying, "Those of us who would rather not be men shouldn't come to practice on Monday, and those of us who do show up don't need to be late."

Monday came. Most came. None were late.

Coach Peters began by telling them that they had seen a side of him on Friday that he hoped they would never have to see again. He said that over the weekend he had reflected on how he had acted and determined he owed each and every one of them an apology. He looked them in the eye and told them he was sorry.

Peters also said he had played the game over and over in his mind and come to another conclusion. The conclusion he came to was that it wasn't their fault that they'd lost the game, it was his. "It's my fault that every damn one of you are chicken shit and out of shape. That's my fault. But starting today I'm going to make it up to you."

And, yes sir, he did.

Move over, Bob Knight.

Breaking The News

*"No matter what you're presenting, how you wrap
the package makes a lot of difference."*

A family sent their daughter off to college. They decided to make a deal with her not to interfere with her new time of independence. "We won't be the first to call or write or visit. We will leave that entirely up to you."

As you might imagine, they didn't get a call or letter the first week, nor the second, nor the third or fourth. After seven or eight weeks the first letter came.

Excited, they sat down at the kitchen table and began to read.

Dear Mom and Dad,

I'm sorry I haven't written before but a lot of things have happened since I arrived at school. Let me start at the beginning. The first week we had a fire in the dormitory. Not a big fire, but those of us on the third floor had to jump out of our windows. You know ole accident-prone me, I hit my head on a ledge and was knocked unconscious. A man named Ed from the filling station across the street picked me up and took me to the hospital. I was OK but they decided to keep me a couple of days for observation and said the blackouts would probably stop, maybe even before all my sight returned. Ed came to visit me and was nice enough to spend the night. After I was released he asked me out and I felt obligated and I accepted. Well, one thing has led to another, and I've decided to move out of the dorm and in with Ed, but don't worry, we're not getting married. He's quite a bit older than I am, and besides, he's still married to his second wife.

Speechless and wide-eyed, they looked at each other and, with trembling hands, they turned the letter over.

I hope all of this hasn't caused you and Dad to go into shock. None of it's true. There was no fire, there was no accident. Ed is a doctor's son I met at a fraternity party. We've been out a couple of times. I hope he will ask me out again, but I have no plans to move in with him or marry him.

I just thought I would have a little fun with my first letter home. I love school, I love you, and I can't wait to see you Christmas.

Your daughter, Bitsy

P.S. I flunked math and got a D in English.

No matter what you're presenting, how you wrap the package makes a lot of difference.

We Have Met The Enemy and He Is Us
— Pogo

*"When political enemies or reporters seemed to have him cornered,
Roosevelt would resort to a story, just like Lincoln before him."*

I have a small bust of Franklin D. Roosevelt on my desk – a symbol of another time who was either loved or hated by just about everybody, and either credited or blamed for just about everything – and a symbol of our time when we're doing just that to somebody else.

FDR's sense of humor was legendary. When political enemies or reporters seemed to have him cornered, Roosevelt would resort to a story, just like Lincoln before him.

My kind of guys.

Roosevelt was once asked why he didn't respect the public's opinion on a certain issue. The President responded with the following story.

> A man was awakened one morning by his alarm clock at the usual time of 5:55. He suddenly realized that it was his birthday. He was 55. Today was the 5th of May. When he opened his mailbox he was reminded that he lived at 555 5th Avenue. This incredible series of coincidences caused

him to do what any of us would do, he called his bookie. "Give me $5,000 on the 5th horse in the 5th race," he almost shouted into the phone.

"Yes sir," was the reply, "but don't you even want to know his name and the odds?"

"Ok, give them to me."

"Lucky Five and he's five to one."

"Call me at 5 o'clock on the dot," our man instructed the bookie.

At exactly 5:00 that afternoon, the phone rang. The news was brief. "5th."

Our man's reaction was brief as well. "Roosevelt, that S.O.B."

The next time you feel like you might want to take to the streets and rant and rave about somebody who's responsible for the state you're in, you might want to glance in the mirror on your way out the door.

AND ANOTHER THING – IN FACT – 50

I believe you'll work out ...

11. Promote from within and hire stingily – work will spread over the workforce no matter how big it is. If a guy named "Hiram Green" shows up, hire him. It's much easier to teach someone than to "unlearn" them.

12. Let all your key employees participate in both profit and equity.

13. Under promise and over deliver.

14. I hear, I forget. I see, I remember. I do, I understand. The only way to train someone is on the job. Learning without doing is what's wrong with our educational system.

15. Always look for people who want to succeed over those who need to.

Brevity Is The Best Teacher

"I was in undergraduate study for seven years. Those are the only three things I remember."

One of my favorite Mark Twain quotes is, "If I had had more time I would have written a shorter letter." The Gettysburg address was written on the back of an envelope, and the Lord's Prayer can be recited in 30 seconds.

John Drewry, dean of the Henry Grady School of Journalism at the University of Georgia, had a unique way to get his point across. Dean Drewry would walk into class, make his point, dismiss the class and walk out. He did that in my presence on three occasions. I was in undergraduate study for seven years. Those are the only three things I remember.

1. Print is infallible.
2. The number one reason people buy is because they were asked.
3. Women spend 85% of the money in this country and directly or indirectly influence the man in spending much of the other 15%.

However, a friend of mine who lives on Florida's emerald coast near Destin may take the prize for succinctness. The O.J. Simpson trial seemed to last about as long as my college career. During the trial I called my friend just to see how he was doing.

"I'm hooked on this damn trial," he said. "Some days I can't even leave the house."

"What do you think?" I asked.

"Well, if you ask me, I think they've framed a guilty man."

Mark Twain, Abraham Lincoln, and Dean Drewry are all alive and well in my friend's house on the Redneck Riviera.

The Lot Is Full

"I'm a catcher."
"Oh!" I said, somewhat surprised,
"I didn't know they had a baseball team."
"No," he laughed, "I'm a chicken catcher."

In the last 50 years, I've met some very interesting and unusual individuals with some very interesting and unusual occupations. A few come immediately to mind. A chiropractor whose favorite patient was a duck. Another chiropractor who specialized in adjusting bulls at artificial insemination farms. A fruit fly feeder, a professional bow and arrow carp shooter, a certified gourdologist – who certifies a gourdologist?

Where's "What's my line" when we need it?

However, my most memorable experience with unusual occupations came in a small town outside of Gainesville, Georgia, when that part of north Georgia was the self-anointed "Broiler Capital of the World", as in chicken.

I had made a successful sales call and was filling out a credit application. After getting the couple's name and address, I came to the section on occupation and income.

"Where do you work, sir?" I asked.

"Jessie Jewel," he replied.

"Is that the chicken processing plant?"

"Yes sir."

"What is your occupation?"

"I'm a catcher."

"Oh!" I said, somewhat surprised. "I didn't know they had a baseball team."

"No," he laughed, "I'm a chicken catcher."

"Chicken catcher?" I said with as straight a face as possible, "Can you give me an approximation of earnings?"

"Four dollars and seventy-five cents a thousand," he replied with obvious pride.

My spirits immediately sagged. Based on my prior chicken catching experience – about one per morning – he had no chance of qualifying for credit, and my sale just flew the coop. But before I could try to pack up and leave gracefully, he continued.

"I know that sounds like a lot," he said, "but it ain't as easy as it looks. As long as the lot's full, I've got the best job down there, but late of an evening when they start getting thin on me I work for my money."

I finished the application – which, incidentally, passed with flying colors – and I came away with a valuable lesson.

Since then, I've always tried to look at life's lot as being full. I think as long as I keep looking at it that way, I'll catch more than my share and I'll have the best job down here.

Persistence Pays, But Know When To Move On

"When I hooked Ladue up to our 200-decibel test unit,
he came alive like Lazarus."

A perky little Girl Scout who had broken several sales records selling cookies was asked how she did it. "By being persistent," was her answer. She was then asked to give an example and didn't hesitate for a second.

Last week I knocked on a door and a great big man with bushy eyebrows – you know, the kind that kind of grow together – answered and asked me what I wanted.

"I'm selling Girl Scout cookies," I replied.

"I don't want any," he said.

I asked if he had ever tried our Thin Mints. He said he didn't want any.

"How about Tagalongs?" I tried, I mean, everybody likes peanut butter.

"I said I didn't want any," he answered.

"I'll bet if you tried the Samoas you'd want some. You know, chocolate and coconut?"

"Young lady," he barked, "I said I don't want any cookies period."

"Do you have some friends that would like some cookies?" I offered.

"I don't have any friends," he growled.

Then I looked him straight in the eye and said, "I'll be your friend if you'll buy some cookies."

While I never sold Girl Scout Cookies I did try to sell myself to numerous girls, but my first official sales job involved hearing aids. I had just turned 18.

I was given the names of the deaf and near-deaf prospects around my hometown. The company's rationale was that a prior relationship might be of benefit.

My career lasted until prospect number four turned me down. The first three knew me just well enough to know that I was totally unqualified, and I never got to first base (see above girl reference).

Number four was a tobacco farmer named Ladue Pardue. I had worked on his farm and knew both Ladue and his wife, Bessie – universally referred to as "Bossie" even by him.

Ladue had not been able to hear himself fart for ten years. He was the perfect prospect, and I had already spent my commission on my latest heartthrob. (see above girl reference again).

When I hooked Ladue up to our 200-decibel test unit, he came alive like Lazarus.

I immediately went for the jugular by filing out the order form and asking if he would be paying by cash or check (credit did not exist in those days).

His reply broke both my spirit and me. "Neither one," he said. I tried to recover by asking him if he could hear. "You bet," he replied. Re-energized I got up enough courage to ask why he didn't want a hearing aid.

No reply was necessary. He simply cut his eyes toward the kitchen.

It was time to move on.

You Can't Hide

"There are defining moments in every life, and deciding not
to deal with any more horseshit was one of mine."

W ill Rogers was supposed to have said that a man who
falls in love with his job is the luckiest man in the
world, because he'll never have to work again. When
I was writing this, I couldn't find his exact quote, but if he didn't
say it, then I will. It's true.

My father was an elementary, middle and high school principal
all at the same time for 41 years. In addition he taught physics,
government, drama, and driver education. He also found time to
coach basketball and work a summer job. He never made $10,000
in a year.

When I was recruited to play college basketball at Wake Forest,
the legendary coach Horace "Bones" McKinney told me that I
was a little small and a lot slow, but he still thought I could play
because I wasn't a "hider." He explained that "hiders" disappear
when the game is on the line. I have never forgotten that, and no
matter what the circumstance I have tried not to hide. And I've
seen plenty who do.

When I graduated from college, I landed a teaching and
coaching job for $6,000 per year, which included seven classes,
the basketball head coaching position, assistant in football and
baseball, and head golf coach. I also drove the athletic bus, and,
along with three other coaches, took care of the gym floor, the

football field and baseball diamond, and oh yes, the laundry for jerseys and uniforms.

I guess I should mention that I ran one of the largest sales organizations in my company and earned three times my teaching salary.

Since I didn't have enough to do, I signed up for a Napoleon Hill night course 70 miles away. The course started at midnight on Mondays and ran for 17 weeks. I received a perfect attendance award.

The straw that finally broke this camel's back came in and around the annual spring horse show benefit for our band. The coaches were assigned field maintenance and clean up. There are defining moments in every life, and deciding not to deal with any more horseshit was one of mine.

I did, however, carry the work ethic with me. I already knew that the best prospect to help you do something was the busiest one you could find. That is every bit as true today. I travel 100,000 miles a year, speak to 25,000 people, come to the office every day I'm in town, and serve on seven boards.

A close friend asked me to get involved in a project with him. I told him that I was extremely busy. His reply caused me to change my mind. "If you want a really tough job, try doing nothing for a while."

Did I mention I'm writing a book?

A Man Who Understood

"Somebody's got to even things out a little," he used to say.
"Folks won't do it by themselves."

If I had to summarize my father's life with one phrase it would be that he was "a man of understanding." He understood where he came from, who he was, and, most importantly, where he was going.

His father was an only child – the son of a horse-trading Baptist preacher who fought in the Civil War. He grew up on a small farm near what is now the West Yadkin School. There were nine in the family. My father was the second youngest and last to go. He understood what it was like to lose a father. His died when he was ten years old.

My father understood what it means when a family pulls together in time of need. He often told of how his older brothers and sisters helped the younger ones, left fatherless at home. He idolized his older brother, LeRoy, who took him under his wing and kindled his interest in education and sports – and later politics.

He understood what it was like to have very little, and work for everything you got. He never wasted anything. I don't believe he ever once left a bite of food on his plate in 90 years. Of course, my mother's cooking might have had something to do with this.

He understood what a real education was all about.

With crops in the field and children to feed, his father sought education as an adult and later became superintendent of schools in Yadkin County.

A Record Unbroken

My grandfather's belief in education inspired my father and all four of his brothers to attend college and later set a record as the only family with five brothers to graduate from Wake Forest. (Daddy used to say that this record may stand forever "because nobody could afford it anymore.")

He understood what it meant to share his education with others and that love and responsibility go hand in hand. Whether it was in the classroom, on the court, or on the stage, he felt personally responsible for his students and players.

Daddy would have rather missed a meal than a class reunion. The Moxley Reunion was the highlight of his social season.

He understood that government works only when people participate.

His heroes were Franklin Roosevelt and Hubert Humphrey.

His causes were public education, schools, gymnasiums, roads, public utilities, Social Security, Medicare and Civil Rights.

"Somebody's got to even things out a little," he used to say. "Folks won't do it by themselves."

The Best Medicine

He understood that laughter was always the best medicine, and he had a pharmacy full.

His all time favorite entertainer was Will Rogers. His favorite ball player was Dizzy Dean, and his best friend was Cliff Wallace.

If folks are sitting around somewhere in the hereafter telling stories – they need to pull up a chair and get ready... my daddy's got a few of his own.

My father understood that this world is a "bigger place than Buck Shoals." He used to tell me if he ever made it to Russia he'd shake the hand of every person in Stalingrad and thank them for what they did during World War II.

He taught physics, but he knew more about history and geography than any textbook I ever read.

Lastly, he understood that there was more to the universe than the world itself.

My father studied biology at Wake Forest under Dr. William Poteat, who later became president of the State Baptist Convention.

A Strong Faith

Dr. Poteat instilled in my father the belief that faith and knowledge were by no means incompatible.

My father was not uncomfortable with the Darwins of his day nor was he with the Hawkings of today.

Knowledge only strengthened his faith, and it was strong to the end.

He told me a few weeks ago that he was absolutely certain that he was heaven bound.

"It does not have to have gold-lined streets – or even be laid out in a square," he said. "If your mother is there, I'll know I'm in the right place."

He was a man of understanding.

We'll all miss him, but thanks to him, we understand.

1973 NSA
BAHAMIAN
CRAB RACE

AUGUSTA
NATIONAL
GOLF
CLUB

Tanglewood

ST ANDREWS LINKS

THE
OLD COURSE

SOUVENIR SCORE CARD

Larger than Life

If I could live forever I
would play in the NBA for the
rest of my life. One reason
for playing basketball is for money.

AND ANOTHER THING – IN FACT – 50

Let's Talk ...

16. Be accessible from morning until night.

17. Serious conflicts involving people can only be resolved eyeball to eyeball.

18. Schedule meetings on the same day, at the same time, in the same place and with no phones. (See church)

19. Design conference rooms so everybody can look at everybody. (See King Arthur)

20. Two heads are better than one. Two-person teams work, even at the top. That's been my model for 50 years. Just make sure you have the right partner – and that he or she does, too.

No Problems = No Opportunities

"Her foot hit the carpet runner and she literally slung two quarts of scalding hot 'to-die-for' gravy into the center of the dining room table."

I can't count the number of times that I've learned and relearned that, without problems, there are no opportunities.

Nowhere was that brought home more vividly to me – served up, if you will – than during my first cookware dinner after I moved to Athens, Georgia. I was working for the West Bend Company, and our method of selling was to demonstrate our line of cookware by actually cooking dinner in the home of a hostess and some invited guests.

I had booked my first presentation with a lady whose husband owned the local laundry.

She promised to invite four couples, and I promised to cook the most delicious meal they'd ever eaten.

My next job was to find an assistant to help with serving and tidying up. I placed a call to the dormitory on the Georgia campus in Athens, spoke with the girl on the switchboard, and explained what I needed and what I would pay. Her response was that she would like to help me, and that she was available Saturday night – available Saturday night being my first indication of trouble.

At that time in my life I couldn't exactly go through a screening process. My net worth consisted of about $300 in cash and a set of pots and pans that I desperately needed to unload.

Saturday night came and I picked her up at the dorm, and my

suspicions as to why she would be available were immediately confirmed.

On the way to the dinner party she dropped another bombshell, admitting that she had zero kitchen experience, with a capital Z.

When we arrived, I couldn't say that she wasn't actually with me, but I could at least hint that she was not my wife, my fiancée, nor my date. Or my sister, my cousin, or my parole officer. I couldn't come up with any reason why she was dressed like she was, or what she had done to her hair.

The meal preparation went well; the crowd was great and included some good prospects except for the Methodist minister. He asked for a discount before I mentioned the price.

The hostess had set a beautiful dining room table, and after the blessing and before the request for a discount, we began the serving process. My routine was to serve the meat and potatoes and have my assistant follow with a "to-die-for" gravy. I had instructed her to stay close to me to make sure nobody ate before the food had been properly doused. I waited, and waited some more, and finally she appeared, trying to juggle two quarts of scalding hot gravy in a stainless steel bowl using one paper towel.

This was, of course, a recipe for disaster, but no one could have predicted the catastrophic size of same. Her foot hit the carpet runner, and she literally slung two quarts of scalding hot "to-die-for" gravy into the center of the dining room table. At that instant, some law of physics took over and the gravy exploded like a grenade. We're talking carpet, laps, glasses, curtains, and everything else within a 25-foot radius. Including the dog. All I could do was go totally silent.

The laundry man said he would clean the clothes and curtains, but looked at me and said "I'm not cleaning the XXXXXXX carpet. Sorry, Reverend." The dog was on his own.

I finally broke the ice with a comment, "You've got to try this gravy."

After that, things went pretty smoothly the rest of the night.

On the way back to the dorm I tried to console my "former" employee, but nothing seemed to work. Finally I said, "Look, we'll be telling grandchildren about this years from now, every time gravy is served, or anybody spills something on a carpet." That along with a tip and telling her that she might consider culinary arts as an elective brought a nice smile. I saw her a few times on campus after that – during the week.

The next day I took $75 of my $300 and rented a carpet-cleaning machine for the first and last time in my life. The carpet was lime green, and the gravy spots made it look like chocolate mint ice cream. Once I cleaned the dining room, by comparison, the rest of the carpet in the house looked like it had been laid 50 years ago, and by the time I finished the entire house, I looked worse than that. And both of us, carpet and me, were unraveling.

The following day I was back on sales calls.

My first prospect was the chief surgeon at Athens general hospital. In spite of his demanding occupation, he had still managed to father nine children. When I arrived, he met me at the door with a big smile and said he had some good news for me. His wife had decided they needed two complete sets. I almost fainted. My net worth and my cash had just doubled in five minutes. However, he was not through, "You also need some help," he said, "and I have some for you. Judy, come here." Out walked an absolutely gorgeous 15-year-old with a "to-die-for" smile that would light up an entire city. "My daughter Judy needs a job and, trust me, she knows her way around a kitchen."

Judy, you might say, was the gravy on the deal.

For the next three years I enjoyed the company of the absolute antidote to my previous one-night stand. She was perfect, and together we built the largest organization in the company.

There are no opportunities without problems. Thank you, Judy, wherever you are.

And pass the gravy.

One Angry Man

"He said we pay insurance so we can get our cars fixed, not so we can listen to Almeda bitch and moan every day."

A guy that I knew by the name of Joe Moss had to be the most obstinate individual ever conceived, if, in fact, he was conceived. He drove a new Cadillac every year, ran a store, owned rental property, and never even bothered to apply for a driver's license, nor did he ever file a tax return. He defied federal and state governments, tickets, court orders, audits, and even a threatened prison sentence or two.

Take this story, for example. Once Joe's neighbor decided to get into the hog raising business and constructed a lot adjacent to, and upwind from, Joe's property. Joe decided to take his neighbor to court. After hearing the evidence, the judge told Joe that, while he sympathized with him, there was no law or zoning restriction that prohibited the neighbor from raising hogs on his own farm.

Joe's response was immediate. "Your Honor," he asked, "Is there any law against a feller raising sick hogs?"

"Not that I know of," replied the judge.

Within a week or two the smell was gone.

A woman who knew Joe quite well told me another story that epitomized Joe. She was serving on a jury with him, and after the final arguments were heard, and the judge charged the jury, the foreman asked for an initial vote. The tally was 11-1 in favor of the defendant.

The lady said that she immediately started praying that the "1" was not Joe because, "We'll be here six months." Then the foreman asked who the dissenter was and, sure enough, it was Joe. One juror switched his vote immediately, citing that he was expecting his first grandchild in the fall. Another juror asked Joe what it would take to convince him and Joe replied "nothing," at which point juror 6 switched with no explanation. After just one afternoon of balloting and deliberation, the foreman declared that they had finally reached a unanimous verdict in favor of the plaintiff.

I asked the lady if she could tell me what the case was about.

"Just a wreck," she said. "This lady was driving along and a bee got in the car. She got so rattled that she ran through a stop sign into the banker's wife's car, which was parked in a no parking zone. We felt like the banker's wife should get a ticket but Ida Faye was driving the car and was the one at fault."

"What was Joe's reasoning?" I asked.

"Well, Joe saw it different. He pointed out that Ida Faye's husband was a drunk, and she didn't have any insurance, and because of this wreck she was having to ride to work and everywhere else with Almeda Thompson, who would drive a psychiatrist crazy. On the other hand, Mrs. Creedmore (the banker's wife) had all kinds of insurance, and her husband would figure out a way to make a profit out of the whole deal. He said we pay insurance so we can get our cars fixed, not so we can listen to Almeda bitch and moan every day. I think it was all of us knowing Almeda that turned it around."

Angry logic.

Redneck vs. Mountain Man

"He was a big ole certified, wife-beater-wearing redneck and his demeanor was big ole certified, vein-popping red ass."

I taught and coached in Georgia with a guy whose address was Star Route, Bee Log, North Carolina. He was, in every sense of the word, a mountain man. We called him "Doctor."

One day he walked into the teacher's lounge and announced he had failed a certain student in PE. A hush fell over the gathering. Then one of the teachers spoke up, "I'd get my things in order if I were you." Others followed. "His daddy is the meanest S.O.B. in this county." "You won't live a week," etc. Doctor calmly took off his size 55 coat and said, "Well, we all have to go sometime or nother."

Next day, the meanest S.O.B. in the county called and said he'd be up to talk later that afternoon. Doc drafted me and another coach to post ourselves outside the door to the coach's office "in case fur starts a flyin'."

R.L. arrived in a muffler-less pickup covered in Wallace stickers. You pick your own contemporary equivalent. He was a big ole certified, wife-beater-wearing redneck and his demeanor was big ole certified, vein-popping red ass.

The discussion centered on R.L.'s insistence that his son's grade be changed from an F to an A and the good Doctor's unwillingness to change it even to an F+. Finally, to the delight of the peace-loving, scared-stiff sentries, Doc proposed a compromise.

"R.L., I'll make a deal with you. Whatever Eddie makes the next six weeks I'll go back and change his grade from this six weeks to whatever that grade is."

Sounded more than fair. Didn't sound that way to R.L.

His response was, "Awright, now I've gotta deal for you, big boy. If he makes an A next time and you give him an A this time then I won't come back up here. Anything less, I'll be back and you don't want me back. Understood?"

Doctor was quick to respond, "I gotcha," he said. "And I'd sure hate to see you have to drive all the way back here so I'm just gonna go ahead and whip your ass right now."

R.L. swallowed a nice chaw of Red Man. Case closed – the mountain man prevailed. We need more doctors.

Call It Luck Or Call It Fate,
Or Call It A Full Moon

*"In other words, the moon or Jupiter or something very wide
and white was out at 11 in the morning."*

When I graduated from the University of Georgia I moved to Augusta to begin my teaching career, which lasted two years - my first and my last. I taught them both in the same nine-month period.

Having agreed to a salary of not very much per year supplemented by a lot less for also coaching, it was imperative to get my fire alarm business off the ground and running before school started.

My first move was to run an ad in the paper for potential sales people. As you might imagine, Murphy's Law entered the picture and the phone company didn't come through with my installation, so I was forced to put the number of the phone booth outside the laundromat in my apartment complex in the ad.

The initial ad response was good and in spite of the July heat – and having to explain to a few prospects that I was not in a phone booth, as in "the air conditioner in my office is on the fritz and my windows were open, that's why you hearing traffic" – I was able to hire a decent number of sales people.

My big break, however, came almost a month later.

I was washing my clothes at the laundromat when the phone

outside rang. For some reason I decided to answer. Force of habit. Lo and behold it was someone calling from my ad a month before. I instantly went through the spiel and wound up hiring the first guy to make it all the way to the top of my organization.

Luck? Fate? Both?

Almost 40 years later, I was driving around surveying the damage of Memphis's worst natural disaster in recent history "Hurricane Elvis." Elvis was a straight-line wind of 100 MPH that cut a mile-wide swath through the center of our city leaving hundreds of thousands without power and a massive cleanup problem.

I was in the section of Memphis we call Midtown and had stopped at a police roadblock. Suddenly my eyes caught a glimpse of an unusual sight in the upstairs window of a house on my right. It appeared as if a rather large woman was sitting or standing in the window with nothing on her rather large bottom. In other words, the moon or Jupiter or something very wide and white was out at 11 in the morning.

I was soon motioned to move on, and when I returned on purpose an hour or so later the moon had disappeared.

A month or so later my company was in the process of moving, and we were looking for someone to either sell or give our used furniture to. A friend suggested I talk to the Church Health Center, a faith-based organization that provides medical service to the working poor.

He gave me the address and the name of Dr. Scott Morris, the head of the center. When I arrived, I was shocked to see the address was the same house where I had witnessed a near total eclipse.

I was so impressed with Dr. Morris and the work they were doing, (The Church Health Center has 60,000 patients of record and offers them health coverage for under $50 per month), I gladly gave him all of our furniture and asked if there was anything else we could do.

Dr. Morris immediately asked if I knew how he might be able to obtain a generator. He then told a story of a rather large woman who had come to his office during the aftermath of Hurricane

Elvis when the power was out and everything went dark. He said she had a boil in a rather difficult place to see, and he had to ask her to stand in the window to give him some more light. Turns out, we both saw it.

In fact, we did have a generator, Scott and I have become the best of friends, and I proudly serve on the executive board of the Church Health Center.

Luck? Fate? Both?

I'll leave you with this, a full moon shines nine times brighter than a half moon.

I Remember

*"How many years can some people exist before
they're allowed to be free?"* Bob Dylan

It's always the little things you remember.

Like my grandfather... who was a school superintendent and road horseback all winter in the snow to fill a campaign promise to teach one day in all 64 one-room school houses in his county. Yet he lived at the foot of "nigger" mountain, and once spanked me for drinking from a "colored" water fountain in Sears & Roebuck.

Like my daddy... drinking from a black farmer's dipper and looking at me like I better drink too or there would be trouble when we got home.

Like me... the first time I said the "N" word, and the bitter taste of lava soap in my mouth afterwards, though not nearly as bitter as having to swallow hard and apologize to Delia, our housekeeper, whose love I cherished and returned.

The little things that turn out to be big things after all.

Like seeing our best player dragged off the basketball court by his father because my father had simply scheduled a scrimmage game with the all black high school prior to segregation.

Like hearing about the great Oscar Robertson being forced to stay in a separate hotel when he became the first black player to play against white players in North Carolina.

Like reading about the number one basketball team in the

nation, Mississippi State, being barred from playing in the NCAA tournament by their state legislature because they were scheduled to play against blacks.

Like being asked by a 10th grader during the first year of integration, and my first year as a teacher, if I thought it was okay for her to ask a black classmate to accompany her to a dance.

Like my father retracing a bus route – just to remind himself, and especially me, that it was a total of 64 miles that uncle "Teen" Blackburn's 11 children had to ride a bus every day to a black school when they could have walked to a white one.

Like the night Martin Luther King was assassinated and my friend and I drove to the black area of Athens, Georgia, and simply walked around and hugged everybody we met.

Like the night Barack Obama was elected and the day he was inaugurated.

I remember and I will not forget.

Professional advice should be taken advisedly ...

21. One lawyer is better than none.

22. Accountants should give you the bad news yesterday and save the pleasant surprises for tomorrow.

23. Computer programmers have a language all their own. It starts with yes equals no. They're dangerous because they actually believe what they tell you.

24. Consultants want to borrow your watch to tell you what time it is. I would advise all aspiring consultants to call themselves "resultants" and get paid accordingly.

25. Marketing is where it all happens. Good marketing makes sales almost superfluous. (See Starbucks)

We Are All Dumb, Just On Different Subjects

"As you might expect, 'Silent Night' was not on the German II final. F was."

When I arrived at Wake Forest College in the fall of 1961 I was asked to choose my most likely major. Since at one point during a particularly good Perry Mason episode I had thoughts of being a lawyer, I chose political science.

I soon learned that a major in political science required six semesters of a foreign language. Having taken two years of high school French, during which I learned to count to ten, conjugate to be, say "How are you?" and sing "Frère Jacques," I found out I might start with the second or third semester. All I needed to do was take a placement test.

The instructions for this test were in French as was the person administering it. I was able to decipher about 10%, which was exactly the percentile ranking I achieved. My reaction was to leave France for my first semester and see what developed.

During that semester I learned that the Spanish department at Wake Forest was "basketball friendly," and my best bet was to forget French and learn to sing the malaguena. I was later to learn that the malaguena has no words. And it's a dance.

My first class was taught by an eccentric, gesturing, r-rolling professor who believed that speaking Spanish was the key to learning Spanish, so our class was one continuous language lab. I was so excited about this approach I forgot to even purchase the vocabulary and grammar textbook, and wound up with a "basketball friendly" D. Spanish II was a total disaster three times, so when I was asked to leave school, I did so with that D in Spanish I and a new major, which required only two semesters of foreign language. One more to go.

I immediately found that the University of Georgia Spanish department couldn't care less whether or not I'd played basketball at Wake Forest, and I was greeted with my fourth F in Spanish II in as many tries. I'm nothing if not consistent.

During my third junior year, I almost got a break when my roommate and I walked into our favorite beer parlor (there were a few close seconds) and, after zwei pitchers each, joined in with a German choral group. The "director," who was also a German professor, was so impressed with our singing (I later sang "Silent Night" in German at the local Lutheran Church) that after pitcher drei, he not only invited us to join the group, but to take both German I and II under his tutelage.

Wunderbar, I passed German I with flying colors and was headed into the home stretch in German II when disaster struck again. Our professor (forever to remain nameless) had been caught for (forever to be sealed) and was forever not allowed to teach German in Georgia. As you might expect, "Silent Night" was not on the German II final. F was.

I was down to my last pitcher. Since I was always at my best under pressure, I decided to do what I should have done six years before. I took Spanish I over, got a better foundation, and made it through Spanish II just in time to graduate.

I must, however, give credit to a certain Spanish professor, who shall remain nameless, that I dated during those two last semesters of my 2nd senior year. I will never give you up, Alice, I promise.

Gracias.

Just Relax

"My doctor is 6'10" in surgical sandals, hands the size of stop signs, perhaps a sign we should stop this whole thing right now."

I know prostate checks are absolutely necessary, especially when you get to be my age, but that doesn't make you look forward to them with any increasing degree of delight. My experience in this area has been, I guess, for the most part typical, but nevertheless worth sharing, at least with my fellow males over 50. Actually – it's worth telling – I'll let you and your doctor share it.

My doctor is 6'10" in surgical sandals, hands the size of stop signs, perhaps a sign we should stop this whole thing right now.

His office is standard – crowded waiting room, old magazines, small, cold examining rooms, and a 30-minute to all-day wait – both in that waiting room reading Field and Stream from some year before the big war or sitting on a cold, hard, steel table waiting for… the examination.

The routine is routine. "Mr. Albert Martin," my first name, not the name I go by. "This way, sir. Please remove your shirt," and hang it over there with most of your dignity, "the doctor will be with you shortly," shortly being defined as anywhere between actual shortly and far more than longly.

I follow orders. I sit, I stand, I sit again, I look around, the diplomas are in order, and… oh no, why did I look… there it is, that box of rubber gloves… one gross, clear XXXL, and there it is... the tube of KY Jelly, rolled into a literal knot with maybe one more squeeze left, if it'll break through the crust... and then the final alarm, the high school basketball team photo with "Ole Doc," obviously the leading rebounder, front and center palming two basketballs at no more than 15 years of age.

In comes "Ole Doc," and the game begins.

"How are you, Albert?" he asks as he shakes my hand and two thirds of my forearm. "Everything OK?" At first he checks enough other things to give you a faint ray of hope that maybe he'll forget this time, or better still, there is a new procedure and driving a truck up there and turning on the lights won't be necessary.

Then you know it's coming.

He goes through an O.J. Simpson-like struggle just to get the glove on. He warms up by palming the family jewels and asking you to cough. Then "Ole Doc," the greatest center in Sevierville history, asks you to lean over and "JUST RELAX."

Rough Night

"After all, sex and golf are cousins in the sense that they are, according to an old bartender friend of mine, 'The two most humbling experiences a man can have.'"

Golf is a four-letter word. A round of golf is a series of four-letter words. A golf course is a place where men go to lie about what they're doing, what they did, and what they're capable of. Nothing is out of bounds on a golf course, except, of course, a number of your shots.

Sexual exploits are required topics. After all, sex and golf are cousins in the sense that they are, according to an old bartender friend of mine, "The two most humbling experiences a man can have."

While I was an exception to all these rules and never lied about how long a putt was I made, or how short a putt was I missed, and certainly never discussed my encounters with members of the opposite gender, I was, however, forced to listen to a story from a friend named Roy – responding to a remark by a member of our foursome who said that his latest bad shot was due to a rough night.

By the way, I just lied about those putts.

"One night about fifteen years ago," he began, "I was carrying on with a sweet young thing at my office. We'd gone to a motel after a particularly happy happy hour, and were wadded up in the bed like worms.

"At a most inappropriate time, there came a knock on the door. I looked through the little glass thing to see who it was and didn't recognize the fellow standing there. I tried to disguise my voice anyway just to be safe, and asked him what he wanted.

"He asked if I owned the blue Chrysler in the parking lot. I did, but I wasn't about to tell him. Before I could get 'no' out of my mouth, he said that he'd accidentally backed into my car and needed to give me his insurance information because he was leaving town.

"Like an idiot, I told him to wait till I got my pants on and I'd open the door. When I did, there stood sweet thing's husband, her brother and the lying S.O.B. who'd told me he'd backed into Old Blue.

"A brief scuffle occurred, and the only thing in my favor was the fact that it's hard to miss when you're swinging at three of 'em. They got me subdued pretty quickly, especially after two of 'em held me down on the bed while the other one unzipped my pants with a switchblade.

"They 'asked' me to call my wife and have her join the party or they'd do a little surgery. I said to try not to leave a scar. When they produced alcohol and a sewing needle, I reconsidered.

"When my wife answered I followed instructions and told her where I was, who I was with, and what we were doing (he probably left out the wadded-up-like-worms reference). I then extended her an invitation to come on down. She said she'd see if she could work it into her busy schedule, and five minutes later showed up at the door, having broken whatever speed record existed between our (soon to be her) house in Frayser and the Admiral Benbow some 20 miles away.

"After everyone exchanged pleasantries, the family of the 'bride' left. I begged them to stay and almost asked if I could go, too, but my wife had other plans, and a demand.

"She marched me outside, down the stairs, and out in the parking lot where we saddled up Old Blue and headed to Mumford about 140 miles away, so I could tell my mother about the exciting events that had just had just transpired. I should have gone with the switchblade, scar or no scar.

"Now, boys, that was a rough night. Who's up?"

In Baseball, There's A Name For That

"I was 'Ace,' which sounded good before the season started, but lost some of its luster when we went 0 and 10 with me on the mound."

Why is it just about every baseball player has a nickname? Not all football players do. Only one can be Too Tall. Only legendary basketball players do. Like Magic. Only goofy golfers sure do. And Tiger. Boxers are probably second, but nothing like baseball. It's almost like Dizzy Dean, Babe Ruth, Smokey Burgess, and even Catfish Hunter were named that by their parents.

Of course, we had nicknames on my Boonville High School team. I was "Ace," which sounded good before the season started, but lost some of its luster when we went 0 and 10 with me on the mound.

Some of the names were a little on the cruel side. "Wormy" Hinshaw was our team manager. "One-cu-kree" Reece was our catcher – his father was a ballroom dancing instructor with a speech impediment. "Be-Hap" Poteet, AKA "Mr. Magoo," played third base when his glasses weren't broken.

Our double-play combination consisted of "Cat" Casstevens at short and "Chick" Smith at second – nothing unusual to report here, except the time Chick got in a fight behind second base and the player from the other team dared him to step outside.

"Haggis" Brown was the first baseman. He got his name from the TV show "Haggis Baggis" not from the Scottish delicacy –

actually more of a hot mess than delicacy – but Haggis was a mess either way.

The outfield was classic. "Spado" Speas, named for his uncle the town drunk who had six marriages annulled, was in left. In center, was Larry "Bird Shit" Comer. To get a name like "Bird Shit" hung on you, you had to be in the wrong place at the wrong time. Larry's time came when he was fielding fungos one day, and a routine fly caught him right on top of the head, knocking him cold as a cucumber. While we were administering first aid we noticed this white and green stuff all over his face. At first we thought it might be coming from him, but we soon discovered that is was just good old garden-variety bird poop, but a spectacular specimen. It seems that a lone, and I would guess large, bird had bombed "Bird Shit" just as he settled under that fly ball. Right field was manned by none other than Fred "Headzer" Wilhelm, named for the Kaiser – and because he wore about a size 9 cap. Headzer was also the tight end on our football team. It should be noted here that his nickname came from baseball and just carried over to football, but his ole head played a part there, too. We had to special order him a helmet, all the way from Connecticut, which came only in white. Our colors were black and gold, and we didn't get a chance to paint his headgear before he wore it the first time. When Headzer ran a pass pattern he looked like a giant firefly running through the defensive secondary. We never got around to painting his helmet.

Our opponents had nicknames, too. "Poss," short for "Possum," Poindexter must have hit about 600 against us for a team ten miles away called East Bend. If he was playing dead, he sure looked live enough to us. But our most feared opponent was a guy from Yadkinville, our archrival, named "Ugly" Hutchens. Ugly might have been his real name – it fit like his glove –but either way he was a real nightmare for opposing pitchers.

A couple years before me, there were two brothers on our Boonville team – "Maters" and "Stupe" Matthews. Maters got his name when his class was playing a game where you were required to name a fruit or vegetable that started with the first letter of your last name. Since his name was Matthews, naturally he chose "Maters." Stupe acquired his name because in his own words he was, "stupider than Maters."

After games we always used to go to "Mousey" Morrison's grill for cokes and hotdogs. Mousey never played baseball but had a nickname anyway from the baseball team. He was so short he had to reach up to pat out hamburgers on the griddle. One day he was leaning over getting a coke out of the bottom of one those old time roll-top drink boxes, when his feet slipped, and he went straight to the bottom head first and knocked himself out. Maters and Stupe pulled him out.

We scored that one as a save.

If It Ain't Broke, Don't Fix It

"It was obvious to them that Dickie was struggling,
throwing up brick after mortar-dripping brick."

My father was a school principal and teacher, and the subject and point of many of my stories, but his true love was coaching basketball. The small county I grew up in – 6,000 folks if everybody's home – produced a remarkable number of good basketball teams and, obviously, some good players. Among those was a 6'6", 220-lb. center from the little town of Jonesville – 600 folks if everybody's home and has some guests over – named Dickie Hemric.

Dickie's family had very little desire to see him pursue a basketball career or even a college education. My father and Dr. Spencer Bell, who had roomed together in college, wanted to see Dickie attend their alma mater, Wake Forest College, and play basketball. They were successful in convincing Dickie's family this was the right thing to do, and actually drove him the 150 miles to the campus for his first day of school.

Later that fall, Dr. Bell and my father attended a pre-season practice game primarily to see how their boy Dickie was doing.

One of the first things they noticed was that the Wake Forest coaches had changed Dickie from shooting free throws underhanded to the more modern one-hand release method. It was obvious to them that Dickie was struggling, throwing up brick after mortar-dripping brick.

On the way home, Dr. Bell convinced my father to call Head Coach Murray Greason and try to convince him to let Dickie shoot the old way. The call was successful – Dad was a persuasive guy, even without the threat of a woodshed moment – beyond anyone's wildest dreams. Dickie Hemric became one of the all-time NCAA scoring leaders. More amazing, he held the NCAA record for career free throws (905) for more than 50 years until Tyler Hansbrough passed him (982) in 2009 – playing for another North Carolina school, I might add.

As an aside, legendary scorer Wilt Chamberlain – we're talking basketball here, people, his bedroom claims are an entirely different story – couldn't make a free throw on a bet. He and his coaches tried everything over the long course of his career, but the only thing that ever worked at all was throwing them up there underhanded.

If it ain't broke, don't fix it.

Since everybody's involved, involve everybody ...

26. All decisions need to be made as low in the ranks as possible by the fewest people. Organizational charts don't make decisions.

27. Let your assistant coaches coach or you will soon be short of assistant coaches. Tell them if they don't screw up on a consistent basis to watch you to see how it's done.

28. Focus on what you do and let others do what they do. Diversification and diversion come from the same source. Worry less about how many cooks there are in the kitchen, and more about pissing in the soup.

29. Life is a team sport. The mark of a good basketball team is what the four guys without the ball do on both ends of the court.

30. Create a "title dictionary" and use it. It's important that whoever contacts your company for whatever reason feels that they're talking to someone important.

Conventions From Hell

"With an extra couch, some blankets, pillows, and lots of rum, we created a type of Caribbean-style opium den and hoped for the best."

In the last 50 years, I've organized, attended, or spoken at over 100 of our conventions. Almost all of them have been highly successful with some possible exceptions… make that some serious exceptions.

Like the time 200 of us decided to take a cruise and only 18 showed up for our annual awards banquet. Most of the others were battling seasickness, either in their rooms or in the corridors. The scene was like the train station in "Gone With The Wind."

Another fairly memorable downer – so memorable, in fact, it's another story all on its own – was the year O.J. Simpson was to be our keynote speaker and be introduced as our national product spokesperson. Two weeks prior to his scheduled appearance he committed the crime of the century and, during the convention, he was shown every 15 minutes on CNN being hauled off to jail wearing our corporate logo shirt.

We had a girl "dance" through a plate glass window and fall three stories with barely a scratch, a man lock himself out on a balcony naked for over an hour – no, it wasn't me – and an exhibitionist strip in a crowded restaurant, out run security, dive into a harbor, and somehow elude police. Again, not me.

We've had entertainment that didn't show, and a bunch that shouldn't have.

A Chinese opera singer held one note for 18 minutes and when she received applause for finally finishing, she mistook the rousing reception for an encore request.

Adventurists who had walked to the North Pole showed 30 solid minutes of slides with absolutely nothing visible but ice and snow, then wowed the audience with their return trip over the same terrain.

Second runner-ups included a unicyclist who somehow propelled himself into the fourth row of the audience, and a knife thrower who missed his target so badly it took three stage hands to help him find his weapon. Once found, I think I told him where to put it.

First runner-up belonged to a motivational speaker who tried to break the world sit up record on stage while others were presenting.

First place was a '50s band who was scheduled to do a "family" show to an audience of more than 1,000. Their opening number would have caused Roseanne Barr to call the vice squad, and before we could literally pull their plug, they mooned the crowd and exited our hotel still beaming.

The overall convention prize goes to our 1974 Grand Bahama Island meeting. The host hotel was in a remote area with its own landing strip, so we decided to use charter planes to fly the people in and out. One group was to arrive on a certain day, stay three days, and then the planes that brought in the second group would take them home.

We had just hired an experienced convention coordinator whose only drawback was the fact that he liked to keep all details in his head rather than on paper.

Everything went smoothly until two weeks before the convention when he dropped dead at his desk. Yours truly was pressed into service with the help of an intern, and without any facts or figures regarding the upcoming event.

I should have known that my assistant could be a problem when he asked me to carry a 40-pound tape recorder from one end of the Miami airport to the other because it was "picking his double knits." For those of you who do not know the Miami terminal, that's a distance of roughly from South Beach to Key West.

Once we arrived on Grand Bahama Island, things went fine until the morning of the first day, you know, like a couple of hours later. That morning, I got a call from the convention manager informing me that we had a problem. It seems that Doubleknit had pasted perma-seal stickers advertising the theme of our convention on every spot he could find, including over every painted-on door number.

The Bahamian numbering system, which does not recognize the word sequential, presented a unique complication since the seals could not be removed without taking the numbers off with them.

Two nights later, I received a call at 3:00 AM, informing me of an emergency meeting in exactly one hour. At that meeting I was told that another organization's chartered plane had a mechanical problem, couldn't leave the island, and the entire group couldn't be forced to leave their rooms. Our incoming attendees would be short over half of their allotted rooms. One hundred twenty to be exact. Since the closest hotel was 40 miles away via Bahamian dirt road, and there were only 14 taxis on the island, there was no choice but to stay where we were, rain and all. Did I mention the rain?

By putting everybody that had even the most casual of relationships four and six to the room, we were able to trim the "intensive care" unit total down to 40. Our only alternative for the 40 of them was a parlor room – one parlor room – with a half bath and an adjoining bedroom.

With an extra couch, some blankets, pillows, and lots of rum, we created a type of Caribbean-style opium den and hoped for the best.

On the afternoon of the second day of their convention experience, I found enough courage to drop by and tell them that the plane in question was not going to be fixed anytime soon, and it looked like they were there for the duration.

To my absolute shock, my announcement was met with cheers and applause. Our prisoners were having the time of their lives.

Rum was plentiful, new friendships had been created – and more than likely some children – because they'd even worked out a conjugal sign up plan for use of the bedroom in 30-minute intervals. One couple had even given 15 minutes of their time to a couple on their honeymoon.

Moral: Behind every perma-seal sticker there's a room number.

Footnote: Doubleknit was arrested for possession of pot. We bailed him out at the last possible second on the way to the airport. He is no longer with us.

Juice Plus+® Juice Minus

"This gave us adequate time to commit his likeness to every piece of marketing support material and packaging we had, and it gave 'The Juice' enough time to commit the crime of the century."

Juice Plus+® was born out of the juicing craze in the late 1980s. Jay Kordich, better known as the "Juice Man," starred in the most successful infomercial in television history. The popularity of that 30-minute wonder even earned juicing a segment on Saturday Night Live in which Dan Aykroyd juiced a bass. During that time, I was in Seattle one Sunday morning channel surfing and, until I realized I had the remote upside down – bass-akwards, if you will, it seemed as if the "Juice Man" was on every channel at the same time. Remote or no remote, I was impressed and did what millions of others did – I bought a juicer. Again, like millions before me, I juiced twice – my first and last time. I simply did not want to be healthy that bad.

It was in that context we were approached by a homeopathic doctor by the unlikely name of Humbart "Smokey" Santillo.

Dr. Santillo had run across a way to dry fruits and vegetables at low temperature over a long period of time without destroying the nutritional essence. By combining the process with a formula he developed, and adding back some things like fiber that might be lost in the juicing process, and encapsulating the product, he was certain that when taken with a glass of water, you would have a more nutritious, less expensive, more convenient alternative to juicing.

With my usual razor-sharp insight, I immediately turned the idea down, but cooler heads around me prevailed, and we decided to do some testing to determine if Smokey was real hot stuff or just blowing smoke. The testing proved his theory to be feasible, and we launched the product in April 1993.

The launch was low-key – like take a couple of these every day and let us know what happens. The first consistent feedback was in the area of regularity, and a lot was happening. Not since Beethoven and Elvis had as many people been as excited about movements in general and from the waist down specifically. We were excited as well, but just couldn't see how we could build an international marketing effort around this.

At the same time, our manufacturer was trying to get us to try some celebrity spokespeople. The ex-Olympic decathlon champion, Bill Toomey, headed up their marketing department, and he would send celebrities like Nadia Comaneci and Bart Conner and Bob Beamon to our meetings to see if we could find the right fit. While they were all impressive we just could not seem to create the chemistry we felt we needed to take Juice Plus+® to a higher level. One morning I got a call from Bill, who was as excited as he was when he cleared the pole vault in his final jump to win the gold in Mexico City.

"I have your man, I have your man, I have your man."

"Who?"

"Juice."

"Juice Who?"

"The Juice."

"The Juice Who?"

"O.J. Simpson."

Really?

"Yes, he's perfect and he wants to do it."

"Fantastic – can we afford him?"

"I think so. I've set up a meeting to talk."

"Wonderful, Bill, I believe you're right. I really, really thank you for this."

Move over, Beethoven.

The negotiations went remarkably well. We signed a contract and put together a six-month strategy of photo shoots and filming, culminating in a convention appearance where he was to be the keynote speaker. This gave us adequate time to commit his likeness to every piece of marketing support material and packaging we had, and it gave "The Juice" enough time to commit the crime of the century. During our convention he was scheduled to address, our "new spokesperson" was shown on every news channel in the world every 15 minutes being hauled off to jail wearing our Juice Plus+® shirt. It did fit, no s _ _ t.

Heartbreak Hotel.

To say O.J. Simpson was a blessing in disguise is, to say the least, laughable. Well, laughable now. However, it did cause us to go in another direction. Because of the feedback we were getting from members of the traditional medical community we began a program of clinical research, something that was basically unheard of in our industry. The results were so impressive that we were able to gain the support of thousands of health professionals around the world, and Juice Plus+® became the largest selling product of its kind on the planet.

Juice Who?

THE RULES OF STORYTELLING

"It needs to be humorous; even death has it's lighter moments."

It needs to be relevant, at least, somewhere in there.

It needs to be humorous; even death has its lighter moments.

It doesn't need to offend anyone, but it might.

Plagiarism is fair game, almost required.

The truth doesn't need to get in the way, but it's a place to start.

Europe Is A Trip

"Italian train conductors cuss out nuns and kick puppies during their days off. They can rip a ticket out of your hand so fast it leaves a paper cut and blood splatter."

Some years ago, my daughter Meredith and I toured Europe. It was our first time on the grand tour. We were gone 17 days, well, 18 if you count what seemed like a whole day standing in line at the airport in Paris between Air Iran and Air Kuwait checking our luggage. The Iran Contra hearings were going on and there was a blockade in the Straits of Hormuz. It was a time of stress in the Middle East.

Seems like just yesterday.

Here are some personal snapshots.

We started in England. The British are exceptionally polite people – especially the cab drivers. Norman Vincent Peale could take a lesson or two in the back of a London hack. And everybody speaks English, the real kind.

I'll say one thing – they sure do honor their military heroes in England. One afternoon we walked by 50 statues, and except for Disraeli, they were all military folks, mostly Navy. I don't ever remember St. Paul being in the service at all, but there are more dead soldiers per square inch buried in the cathedral named for him than there are at Gettysburg.

If I had one criticism of London I'd put in a plug for bigger hotel rooms. After they got both the twin beds, the bathtub and our luggage in our "suite," there just was hardly any room left for us. For $450 a night, I'd liked to have been able to open my suitcase. With inflation, rising prices in Europe, that whole pound vs. the dollar thing and the English snub of the Euro, etc., while the room sizes have remained the same, I imagine the current price for the room would hover around a million of something a night.

Next we took a bus to Dover. The English countryside was lovely even if it wasn't April. The white cliffs are just like they appear in the movies, and you could almost feel that sense of relief those WWII pilots felt when that coastline finally came into view after a night over Germany.

We crossed the channel by Hovercraft to Calais. About the only interesting things there were the old German gun emplacement bunkers. They were so well built that the French couldn't even blow them up after the Germans left. The walls were 16 feet. thick. Too bad for the Germans we landed at Normandy – still the greatest military surprise since the Trojan Horse.

Brussels, Belgium, was next and it was very enjoyable. The city was clean, the hotel room was plenty large and air-conditioned, and the food was great. I didn't have to eat one sprout. It's a shame the country had to be located exactly between France, Germany and England. The big boys just couldn't resist using Belgium as their battlefield. In between wars, they got a few things done. If you are ever in Europe don't miss the Grand Place in Brussels.

Speaking of grand places – note the grand segue – the Cathedral at Koln, Germany, isn't bad either. It took 600 years to build – before union labor. It survived the bombing that virtually destroyed the entire city. The day we were there they were running a lottery on a new Volvo parked right on the steps out front. Oral Roberts could never hold a candle to the boys from Rome when it came to real fund-raising.

As we traveled more in Germany, I thought about what Will Rogers said while touring Europe after WWI. He said he wanted to be on the losing side next time. The "new" Germany is really something. I sat on my balcony overlooking the Rhine at Boppard (pop. 5,000) from 5:00 a.m. to 6:00 a.m. and counted 21 trains and 43 boats. The guide said not to judge by that, things would pick up some after the sun came up.

Although I've not been to Japan, I'm not concerned about the Japanese taking over. They're too busy touring Europe. However, they were taking some pictures of the place – I heard more clicks than you'd hear at a tap dancing audition.

We played a little bridge in the back of the bus to break the monotony of a six-hour drive through the black forest. My partner led out with a 15-minute dissertation on convention bidding including one club, one diamond, the Blackwood Brothers, Goren, and, I think, Donald Trump. Then, halfway through the third hand he finessed himself for the queen of clubs on his way to three down doubled, redoubled, and vulnerable. I never should have redoubled, but it seemed like the thing to do at the time. Michael Jordan scored less points lifetime than our opponents.

But back to Europe…

Next we visited Heidelberg. According to the brochure, that place has been around since 550,000 B.C., or at least somebody called a "Homo Heidelbergensis" has been walking upright around that place since then.

The Romans showed up about a half a million years later, and then along about 1200 or so a castle got built. In 1386, some guy named Kurfurst Ruprecht started a university, Then the town and the castle and the university all got caught in the middle of a war between the "Charismatics" and the "Fundamentalists" of that day and everybody got burned – kind of like the mortgage crisis.

So, in 1649 Karl "Ichan" Ludwig picked them all up for a song – kind of like the bailout. He obtained new financing by taxing the farmers 10% of their wine crop. He rebuilt the castle and even started up the university again as a public relations ploy.

Karl was determined to make the new castle "impregnablecht," which is medieval German for Star Wars. He built all new towers and gates and dug a moat sixty feet deep. To help pay for the whole program, he built a wine barrel that would hold 55,000 gallons. Even Donald Trump doesn't have one of those. He figured this also might come in handy in case his boys got in one of those thirty-year wars and became a little dry mouthed.

This worked out pretty well until Karl up and died and they got into a big argument over who would take over the wine racket. Karl had been so busy building this castle and collecting wine he forgot to have any children.

Well, Louis the XIV of France, who had been building castles, drinking wine and having children all along, figured he was the man for the job and began a hostile takeover. All Louis' troops volunteered immediately for the Heidelberg front. With 55,000 gallons of wine at stake, a Frenchman doesn't need much encouragement.

The siege began, but no matter how hard they tried, those thirsty Frenchman just couldn't get inside that castle. Then one day the son of the gatekeeper, who had no business outside the gate, got himself captured. The gatekeeper, who was also a member of the HSC (Heidelberg Security Council), made a secret deal with the Frenchman to leave the gate unlocked if they would turn his son loose. Late one night, he even gave three Frenchmen a tour of the castle and a peek at the wine barrel, just to let them know he had the key. There may have been some cheese involved, too.

The next night he let all the Frenchmen inside. They killed all the Heidelbergensians – or is that Heidelbergers? – including the gatekeeper and his son, blew up the castle, and drank the wine. All that's left of the castle today are some reconstructed ruins, a big wine barrel, and a mighty good history lesson. There's even a bit of truth in the way I just told it. Still not sure about the cheese.

On to Switzerland, an incredibly beautiful country full of incredibly industrious people and incredibly large piles of the world's money. They utilize every square inch of their available land and make clocks, cheese, chocolate and interest like nobody else in the world. They are also the best bookies on earth.

The two biggest businesses in Switzerland are insurance and banking, both timely and chocolate-coated.

We all know insurance is the oldest form of bookmaking in the world. The house is the insurance companies, or the "tallest buildings in town," betting the players that they will live to a certain age (usually about 41). Players bet the house that they'll die before that age. The only rule is that players may not kill themselves. In these casinos, the player must also give odds.

These are called pre-existing conditions. The player also has "juice" or "vig" working against them. These are called exclusions. We can all place this same bet in Hartford, but we have a choice. In Switzerland, you're required to have life insurance.

Put another way, while making bets through bookmakers is illegal in most of this country, it's illegal NOT to place a bet in Switzerland.

The next tallest buildings in Switzerland are banks. They're the biggest bookies of all. They book people and they book whole countries. They book people by allowing them to have secret accounts. When they die, only the dead person and the bank know the secret number, and the bank does a number on everybody. When a war comes along nobody knows who will win or lose, including the countries fighting, so they all put their money in Swiss banks. The countries that make it through alive get to draw their money out, but since most of the losers, and even the winners, are dead the only real winner is the Swiss bookie – I mean banker.

The peaceful Swiss love a good war.

My uncle told me once that the only difference between a banker and a robber was which side of the bars he was on. Our guide said not to exchange our money at a bank because they charged you a coming fee, a going fee and a staying fee. That's a fee for staying open just long enough to wait on the guy in front of you.

We traveled from Switzerland to Italy along the most fantastic piece of road construction I've ever seen. My respect for Hannibal, his elephants and whoever else went with him increased dramatically. I also gained some appreciation for the Italians, who built a tunnel ten miles long through the Gotthard Pass and the Swiss, who paid for it, and made a little something, I'm sure.

European rail travel is far superior to ours, and their "interstate system" is too. We traveled 4,000 miles and didn't see a wreck or road construction or any potholes. One of the biggest mistakes we ever made in this country was letting our railroad beds deteriorate, and the second was turning our highway system over to big trucks. We'll be "under construction" forever.

After we got into Italy we took a left and headed for Venice. The Venetians must have really been something in their day. They drove some wood piling in a mud bank out in the Adriatic Sea and ended up with a city consisting of 400 islands for subdivisions and 117 canals for streets.

The City of Venice lasted as an independent state for 1,000 years. They were electing presidents – Doges – in Venice 500 years before Columbus. He was elected for life. We, in effect, do the same thing today. We elect ours for four years and just wear them out. If they survive the first four, we just re-elect them for four more and turn up the heat.

It finally took Napoleon to do the Venetians in. The next time around, it'll be a sanitation worker's strike that'll get them. Or mold.

Next was Florence.

Sportswriters and fans have argued for years about who had the greatest baseball team ever – the '61 Yankees with Mantle and Maris, the '76 Big Red Machine with Rose, Morgan, Bench and Perez. My all-time favorite used to be the '54 Giants. The Yankees had no competition in '61, and the Reds' starting pitching was suspect. My Giants could throw Maglie, Hearn and Antonelli at you and bring Hoyt Wilhelm out of the pen. With Willie Mays, Alvin Dark, Whitey Lockman and Monte Irvin they won the pennant going away then whipped the Indians (who won 112 games) four straight in the World Series. My kind of team.

Remember I said used to be, and this brings us back to Florence.

After visiting Florence, I've changed my mind. Without

question the '01 – that's 1501 – Florence Nightingales were the best team ever.

First of all, look at the owners. The Medici family had more money than all the beer bottlers on both sides of the Atlantic – plus – they were willing to spend it for talent.

Their son Lorenzo "The Magnificient" Medici (the players called him "Skip") was the manager. The leadoff hitter was second baseman Lorenzo Ghiberti (back then the leadoff man was referred to as the "door opener"). Batting second was all-star third baseman Eddie Machiavelli. He was the heart and soul of the team. Eddie could speak 53 languages, which enabled him to steal signals and cuss out umpires without being thrown out of the game. He would have understood Yogi Berra and Casey Stengel. One day after Machiavelli put a Venetian's eye out with a particularly hard slide (hence the term "Venetian Blind" – come on, don't tell me you didn't see that one coming), Eddie leaped to his feet and screamed "Bravo Forenzia" – which roughly, very roughly, translates to the end justifies the means. In the third spot, they had Al "Devil" Dante. Dante's blazing speed – he was fast as hell – put the fear of God or at least a stolen base or two, in every opposing pitcher. He could run rings around anybody. The cleanup hitter was none other than Mic (fans in LA and Houston still call him Mike) Michelangelo. Mic was the perennial MVP. He could do it all – hit, run, throw, paint and sculpt. Michelangelo played until he was 89, a record that still stands. Every fan in the world remembers that catch Mic made in the '14 series in Rome while lying flat on his back. There was just no ceiling to his talent. The rest of the line up was not as well-known, but Hank Thompson and Wes Westrum weren't exactly household words either. Phil Giotto was the shortstop. "Flip" Brunelleschi was the catcher, Don Donatello was in left and Sam Ghirlandaio was a real artist with both bat and glove at first base. The bench was deep, and the farm system was terrific, producing such stars as George Galileo a few years later. Georgie Vasari also came along later to manage for the Medicis and was the architect of several championships.

That particular year, the pitching staff was anchored by Lefty Leonardo da Vinci. Lefty won over 1,000 games and was 34 + 2 in

'01 at Florence. The temperamental southpaw fell out of favor with the Medicis over his constant experimenting with new pitches and turned free agent. He was picked up by Rome and later sold to Paris.

Eat your heart out, George and Schotzie – no one will ever assemble a team like Florence again. I mean, they put up statues of all these guys.

Rome was interesting – ancient Rome, that is.

With the exception of the operators of motor vehicles, the current crop of Romans didn't show me a lot.

However, observing the Roman driver is worth the trip, and the insults you get from other Romans will give a lifetime supply. Magic Johnson hasn't had as many assists in his life as the average Roman gets on his way to work (an assist is a move in traffic which leads directly to an accident). They drive as fast as a Fiat will go and brake only in situations where life and death is at stake, or for a tight skirt. They create their own obstacle courses by parking on the sidewalk, in the median and occasionally – about once per 100 yards – in the middle of the street. We had an accident in a cab inside the Vatican. The only regret I have from our entire trip is being out of film at that time. A picture of our driver standing on the hood of the car that hit us and screaming like an insane person would have been a wonderful souvenir. Love the cell phone cameras we have now since no act of lunacy goes unrecorded or unposted.

The ancient Romans were everything you've read about and more. For starters, the Colosseum was totally covered with marble and built in less than eight years. It seated 50,000 and could be cleared in twenty minutes. It had a dome cover in case it rained or got too hot, and they could flood the floor (called an "arena" – Latin for sand) for mock naval battles. The Circus Maximus where chariot races took place seated 100,000. Their super bowl halftime shows must have really been something. That chariot race in Ben Hur is probably the inspiration for modern Roman driving.

These guys were transporting marble slabs weighing thousands of tons across the Mediterranean Sea from Egypt 2,000 years ago. Most of the wall around the city still stands. There were

1,500,000 in Rome then, and there aren't many more than that now. If they don't improve their driving there'll be fewer by next week.

The Vatican and Rome are separate. The Vatican and Italy are separate. The Vatican and the whole world are separate. The Vatican has more money than all of them. If they run a little short, they just take up a collection, or sell a couple of the bazillion paintings they have.

St. Peter's Bascilica and the Sistine Chapel are magnificent beyond words. Enough said.

We took a train from Rome to Genoa. Here we found the antidote to British politeness – the Italian train conductor. The Italian railroad system has got to be the finishing school for New York cab drivers and prison guards. Italian train conductors cuss out nuns and kick puppies during their days off. They can rip a ticket out of your hand so fast it leaves a paper cut and blood splatter.

We drove from Genoa to Nice. The scenery was nice. Nice was nice. The people were nice; the hotel was nice; the food was nice; the shopping was nice; the nieces were nice – Meredith said to add that Nice had some nice nephews – they were not as nice as those nice Nice nieces. Nice was Nice. And the beach and the nice nieces wearing nothing on Nice's nice beach were particularly nice.

Reluctantly, we left Nice and headed for Paris. After a brief dance on the bridge at Avignon we rolled into the "City of Lights."

What a way to end a vacation.

The first thing we did in Paris was buy our hotel. We had put up a little earnest money before we left home so we went ahead and closed her out while we were there.

We started our Tour de Paris at the Arc de Triomphe built for the victorious soldiers of Napoleon, the same arc the allied armies marched through after taking France back from the Third Reich. Down the Champs-Elysees we went. It was decorated for the final day of the Tour de France.

We passed the Place de la Concorde where Louis the XVI and Marie Antoinette faced the guillotine along with 2,000 more of the French nobility, passed the Louvre, once the palace of French kings, today the most famous art museum in the world, where the Mona Lisa resides (acquired, by the way, in that trade for Leonardo da Vinci with Italy).

We turned left up the hill to the Opera House, then back down the hill and out onto the island in the Seine, which was the original city of Paris. There was the Cathedral of Notre Dame built in the 10th century, the most outstanding example of Gothic architecture in the world.

We crossed the Seine to the left bank, past the Sorbonne and the government buildings, through Luxembourg Park, east to the Eiffel Tower.

Ah, Paris. To paraphrase Bogie and Ingrid Bergman from Casablanca, Meredith and I will always have Paris.

And Nice was very nice.

Travel Associations

*"In Britain, things get serious but never desperate. In Ireland,
things are always desperate but never serious."*

In reflecting on the zillion or so miles I've travelled, I can
associate certain words or feelings with the most memorable
cities, for instance:

Helsinki – Let's get drunk and go naked.

Why did I start with Helsinki? Well, nobody ever starts with
Finland, and Finland is an interesting place to visit – they make
everything from cruise ships to mobile phones – and Finland has
an interesting history.

Around the time of the First World War, they whipped Russia's
ass so badly that a Finnish writer remarked that Russia was so big
and we're so small, there are so many of them, and so few of us,
where are we going to bury them all?

The most revered figure in Finnish history is the national poet.
I wondered why until I came to a street corner and noticed that
each street name contained 30 letters and 2 vowels. Try saying
"Mary, Mary, quite contrary," in Finnish.

The national pastime in Finland is hanging out – and I do mean
hanging out – in saunas, or an excuse for drinking, kinda like a
Cubs game. The Finnish archipelago stretches hundreds of miles
to the east all the way to Russia. There are 100,000 islands and

at least that many saunas. On a warm summer day, or a subzero winter day, or any day for that matter, Finns go island "saunaing." It's a Finnish tradition – when visitors arrive, the host family and the visitors all sauna together naked, share a liter of vodka, and jump in the Baltic Sea.

Wonder why the Russian invasion didn't work out?

Anyway, here are some of those associations that help me sort the world, and like the world, they're in no particular order.

Paris – When you think you have it all, Paris has more.
Nice – Nice nieces on nice beaches.
Rome – Where do I drive?
London – Where do I park?
Beijing – Where do I breath?
Stockholm – Where do I start?
Mexico City – Traffic and trafficking.
Sydney – San Francisco South.
Venice – Let's start a glass blowing business when we get home.
New Orleans – When do we eat?
Houston – Is the GPS working?
Miami – Vice.
Barcelona – Gaudi.
Tokyo – Large and Small.
D.C. – Where do I hide?
Munich – Ein more bier bitte.
Dublin – In Britain, things get serious but never desperate. In Ireland, things are always desperate but never serious.
New York City – Still one of a kind.
Las Vegas – My lips are sealed, kinda like Helsinki and the sauna thing.
Montreal – Get over it.
Toronto – Get with it.
Vancouver – Asia East.
Hong Kong – Where do I walk?

Prague – Check.
Memphis – Soul City.

When you travel, pay attention. The images passing by will last a lifetime.

AND ANOTHER THING – IN FACT – 50

The money doesn't come first, t he sale comes first ...

31. Eighty percent of sales will directly or indirectly come from 20% of your people. Don't let the 80% that produced 20% tell you what is wrong with your product, your price, your system, and the world.

32. Everything you say after you have made your point is a form of an apology. Shut up and let them buy.

33. Selling is a process not an event. Don't show up naked at the door. The sale really begins after the customer buys.

34. Don't get ahead of the game. Take Kenny Rogers' advice, "You never count your money when you're sittin' at the table, there'll be time enough for countin' when the dealin's done."

35. Greed is worse than laziness. See the Seven Deadly Sins.

Perception vs. Reality

"When I was in high school, stealing watermelons was almost a course, and stealing them from this one particular farmer was almost required."

I was in Chattanooga a few years back extolling the virtues of our bacteria-static water treatment system. I spend a lot of time extolling virtues like that. After my presentation was finished I opened the floor to questions.

"Will the system remove radioactivity?" was the first question I received.

Having no idea what the answer was, I struggled to say something. Then it dawned on me, "What difference does it make?" I answered. "If you determined your water was radioactive, your first call would be to your doctor, the second to your lawyer and the third to your realtor. We wouldn't be high on that list."

"In fact," now on a roll, I continued, "if our filtering system was bigger than your house, I doubt that you'd drink the water it treated."

I brought it home, "When I was in high school, stealing watermelons was almost a course, and stealing them from this one particular farmer was almost required. Come July, the class began. He hid his field – we found it. He set up a guard post on the only access road – we waded across a river and carried them out.

"One year, he brazenly planted his melons where access was a piece of cake, and when they ripened we descended like turkey vultures. Only this time it was a trap. He'd placed a sign right where he knew we'd enter the field. *Warning, One Melon in This Field is Poison*, it read.

"We'd been defeated. Slowly we retreated, pausing only long enough to change the *One* on the sign to a *Two*. Perhaps we salvaged a tie.

"Does that answer your question?"

Perception is Reality.

Image Is like Soup:
A Cup Is Great, A Tub Is Too Much

"A man of your means should dress like he is a man of means…"

A friend of mine approached me one day and suggested that I consider wearing tailor-made shirts. "A man of your means should dress like he is a man of means," he opined. I absorbed the insult, and agreed to consider the possibility.

A few days later, a package from him arrived explaining what was involved, including an order form and one of the invoices he'd received as an example of cost. After looking at the invoice, I decided that a loan would be involved and that I wouldn't be a "man of means" long if I wore tailor-made shirts. However, one item on the order form caught my eye. My rude buddy's left arm was 2½ inches shorter than his right, or at least his left sleeve was.

When I broke the news to him that I was just not – cut out – for tailor-made shirts, I got a serious crick in my neck trying to line him up and see if he was really was that much on the slant. Seeing no visible evidence, I finally had to pop the question.

"John, is your left arm actually 2½ inches shorter than your right."

"I don't think so. Why?"

"Well, that stuff you sent me on those shirts had you measured that way."

"Oh", he said. "I just have my shirts done that like that to show off my Rolex."

One tub of soup coming right up.

The Stiff Lady

*"I piled on by saying that considering the wrecks, mama, the brother,
his secretary and the water heater, another $150 was not going to make
a lot of difference."*

Awhile back when we were marketers of fire detector equipment, I got caught in a situation in South Georgia that I will never, ever forget.

My regional sales manager challenged me to a contest in which he and I would take a new recruit and each make a couple of sales calls. The team that did the best would then be treated to dinner by the "ranking" member of the losing team.

I was assigned a guy called Red. Red was green in terms of selling, but very enthusiastic thinking I'd be backing him up.

Red was our team's designated driver, and also in charge of prospects. We pulled into a neighborhood and found the folks at home with no problem.

Red introduced me to a Mr. and Mrs. Leon Phillips. Leon was an affable guy and welcomed us in. Mrs. Phillips was the skeptical, standoffish type, especially when it came to me, and also seemed to be suffering from a serious back problem, which rendered her almost motionless. Thus, the "Stiff Lady." Tough to be warm and friendly when you have all the flexibility of a two-by-four.

Our deal was that the new recruit, in this case, Red, would make our presentation, which included showing some slides and following up verbally. All went well and Red finally came to the point of asking for a decision.

Leon responded first for the Phillips family. "Red," he said, "I guess you heard about our wreck?" Red acknowledged that he had, and Mr. Phillips continued. "We don't ordinarily go that way, but because it was raining and the road construction . . . . . ."

We listened as the story unfolded – the politics behind the road construction, the time and cost involved, and the terrible design and workmanship. After about 30 minutes we arrived, along with the Phillips, at a four-way stop that had been recently converted into a caution light that wasn't working. Phillips was aware of this, but the guy in the truck wasn't. Now we got into the gory details. One of them thought the other was dead. I assumed the Stiff Lady. It took the ambulance forever to arrive. They broke Leon's rib getting him on a stretcher. The ambulance ran into a ditch on the way to the hospital. The emergency room was a total nightmare, and they spent six weeks each in the hospital and were now involved in a contested insurance settlement. This gave me ample time to pack Red's sample case and plan an exit strategy.

But the Phillips were just shifting into high gear. Their son had come home from the Navy to visit them and had wrecked their other car. They were being sued since their son had no insurance.

I was now in a three-point stance, looking at the door, when of all people, the Stiff Lady spoke up, adding further chapters. Her mother had just been placed in a rest home, and the Stiff Lady's brother, who was the only other living member of her family, had run off with his secretary and was in Central America headed south. Finally, and at last, we finished the Book of Job with a hot water heater problem.

Once again, I couldn't pull my exit trigger before Red responded.

"Good Lord, Leon," he said, "You all have really had it rough, but let me ask you something. Other than all that, why would you not go ahead and get these alarms tonight?"

I tried to find some words but couldn't, but I didn't need them. "Red," Leon answered, "Other than all that, I guess we could."

Leon was being pleasantly sarcastic. I knew he was. The Stiff Lady knew he was, even able to smile without pain.

Red, on the other hand, considered Leon's comment to be a buying sign.

He proceeded to congratulate the Phillips and ask their opinion as to where and on which walls the alarms should be hung. I piled on by saying that considering the wrecks, mama, the brother, his secretary and the water heater, another $150 was not going to make a lot of difference.

They were buying all along. Early on, the Phillips had determined that I was not with the insurance company. That was key. It seems that it was the truck driver's fault, they were close to a huge settlement, and all that really needed to happen was for the Stiff Lady to stay stiff just a little longer. But they did have a story to tell. All we had to do was listen.

NO, no matter what form it comes in, is still ON backwards.

An Ounce Of Prevention Is Worth
A Pound Of Sure

*If you do the asking in the right way, then "no"
won't be coming your way.*

The first sales manager I worked for was big on answers. He was the consummate counter puncher. He believed when the prospect raised the objection, you'd better damn well be ready with the answer.

Our sales training sessions consisted of dividing ourselves into teams and letting one team give us an objection and the other team overcome it with a close.

I distinctly remember one such session in which my team was faced with the following objection. "We would like to pray about this."

There was an eerie silence on our side of the table. What could we say?

"I'd rather you wouldn't?"

"Can I join in?"

"When do you think you'll have an answer?"

We were not trying to make light of the subject. We just couldn't seem to deal with it.

Then the guy sitting next to me spoke up and taught me one of the greatest sales lessons I ever learned, "I head price off at the pass, so I'd just head praying off, too, in the same way."

He gave an example. "Mr. Jones, this really isn't a monetary decision, it's not something you'll need to pray on, it's just a question of whether you think you'll use it or not."

Get as many objections out of the way upfront before you're put on the defensive. If you do the asking in the right way, then "no" won't be coming your way.

As to success, you'll have more than a prayer.

If I Had A Hammer

"My friend had never felt a natural hammer before,
and certainly not a female hammer."

Afriend of mine went out to buy a hammer.
He walked into a hardware store and to a big pegboard in
the back. On display were a number of hammers. The two
that seemed most likely to suit his need looked almost identical.
However, one of them was $14.75 and the other was $10.25.

Curious, he woke a clerk up and asked him a seemingly
logical question, "Tell me, buddy, what's the difference in those
two hammers?" Appearing dumfounded by the question, the
clerk replied, "Four dollars and a half not counting your tax."

My friend pressed on and went into a second store. Amazingly,
there was not only a very similar display, but the same identical
hammers and the same two prices. Before he could even ask, a
sales person shook hands with him, introduced himself, and gave
him the following information.

"I see you're looking at hammers, and I noticed you're not a
carpenter when we shook hands. No calluses. A carpenter knows
the mark of a good hammer is whether or not she's balanced."

He took the $14.75 hammer off the wall and let it rock on the
claws back and forth, back and forth. "The average sub floorer
nails 28,700 nails a month. He needs something that kinda swings
easy. Give her a grip. Sorta feels natural in your hand, don't she?"

My friend had never felt a natural hammer before, and

certainly not a female hammer.

"That handle's made out of second growth hickory...not first growth...second growth! It'll stay smooth as long as you use it. See those fluted claws, your wife could pull a thumb tack out of a sheet rock wall and never bruise it, or you could jerk up rusted railroad spikes and they'll never snap off. You'll never drive a wedge in that double-dropped, steel-forged head, and, if you were strong enough and could last long enough, you could beat on case-hardened nails in cinder block until your arm broke but the head of that hammer would never pit. Mister, that there's a hammer."

My friend awakened from hypnosis long enough to ask if there was something cheaper.

"Oh sure, came the reply. It ain't balanced, feels like a hockey stick, and the handle's made out of southern pine. You keep it sanded real good and you'll keep the splinters out of your hand. Mostly."

And there's your difference.

If you're going to lead them, make sure they haven't already left ...

36. True leadership is for the benefit of the followers, not the enrichment of the leaders. In combat, officers always eat last. Or the good ones do at least.

37. Sometimes a little mystery is ok, but in the end, openness trumps secrecy.

38. Gut feelings usually trump statistics. Try to decide early and then back yourself into the facts.

39. Don't make business decisions for tax reasons.

40. All opportunities come from problems. It's not just lemonade that comes from lemons, it's something cool and refreshing that came along when things were getting too hot and depressing.

Someday Never Comes

"We're all alike in this family. When the flag drops we're either gonna win the race or wreck the car."

I must confess that I have not read that many business-related – or related to anybody – self-help books. If you think this little exercise of mine is self-help, well then, help yourself.

I did enjoy *Think & Grow Rich* by Napoleon Hill, a couple by Tom Peters that focused on focus, Tom Friedman's *The World is Flat*, and *Up The Organization* by Robert Townsend.

There was a common thread in each of these, and for that matter in the entire genre. Procrastination and indecisiveness are the number one and two enemies of success.

I may be called obsessive compulsive by some, but I have always believed in the old adage, "You never know how soon it will be too late." A good idea needs two ingredients:

First, it needs to be a good idea and, second, not quite enough time.

Bill Russell was the greatest basketball player who ever lived. Oh, there are those who would argue for Michael Jordon, or Oscar Robertson, or Wilt Chamberlin, or LeBron James these days, but give me a break. Basketball is a team sport. Russell never lost a game in high school or college, and won 12 NBA championships, more than all those guys combined. He was also a great TV analyst. Once when a player missed a layup and Russell's partner asked him what happened. "Well," said Russell, "He got to the rim and couldn't decide whether to dunk it or bank it off the glass, so he tried to do both and did neither."

Indecisive.

My son played soccer in grade school and one weekend there was a tournament in Mississippi. It was July and the temperature and humidity were both about a hundred. The luck of the draw, as in bad luck, put our team in a situation to play back-to-back games in the hottest part of the day. During the second game I sat next to a friend whose son seemed oblivious to the heat and was all over the field making plays. I asked my friend jokingly what he was feeding Jesse. "Nothing," was his reply. "We're all alike in this family. When the flag drops we're either gonna win the race or wreck the car."

Decisive.

The problem with the habits of procrastination and indecisiveness is that they're almost impossible to break. To some people tomorrow, next week, next month and next year will still mean tomorrow, next week, next month and next year, tomorrow, next week, next month and next year. I have, however, developed a cure and can testify to its effectiveness.

Get a notebook, and obviously a pen. Place it where you can't miss it, as on your pillow. Each day for a month write down all the "now" decisions you made. The more trivial the better. Duplication is good. Examples would be... put shoes in closet, hung pants up, filled up with gas before the light came on, didn't eat bread or sweets today, etc., etc. You will find the little now decisions will become bigger and bigger until you finally graduate.

The final exam, for example, for a woman might be to call some girlfriend you really should, but really, really don't want to. For a man, it's stopping to ask directions. You'll know when you've passed.

"Well, I'm here to tell you each and every mother's son, you better learn it fast you better learn it young 'cause, someday never comes." – Credence Clearwater Revival

New York City Marathon

"A lady came by me wearing a sweatshirt that exclaimed, 'Your doors have just been blown off by a 71-year-old woman.'"

As a rule, I like people who are passionate. Obviously, there are plenty of exceptions, but my friend, Ron, is not one of them. As the sales manager for our product, Juice Plus+®, you could not ask for someone so in love with his job. He also gets excited about other things that enter his life from time to time. One of these was running, as in marathons, half marathons, 10K's and 5K's and every other kind of K every day for 13 years in a row.

I must have caught some type of bug from Ron because at his insistence, my wife and I committed to run the New York City Marathon with Ron.

The New York City Marathon starts on Staten Island, winds through all five boroughs, and ends in Central Park. We arrived the day before, and Ron appointed himself as our tour guide. He said we should all meet in the hotel lobby at 4:00 AM and walk about two miles to catch a bus that would take us from Midtown Manhattan to Staten Island. I asked what I considered to be a obvious question, "Why so early? The race does not start until eleven o'clock." Ron said that we needed to experience the "atmosphere." The "atmosphere" forecast for early the next day was 18 degrees.

Being Ron's boss, I felt as if I had both the authority and the means to keep this from happening. I told Ron that I had already arranged for a limousine to pick us up at 9:30, take us to Staten Island, and pick up those of us who were still alive at the finish line and take us gently back to the hotel.

While Ron was disappointed, cooler heads prevailed, and the issue was settled without anyone freezing in Staten Island's predawn light.

Enter someone just as passionate as Ron... the limo driver.

This guy didn't just sleep in his limo, he slept "with it." Pat, that was his name, patted and wiped and shined every inch of that baby in a continuous loop. He even got out at a light to remove something from off the hood.

Ron was impressed.

The Marathon went well early, then they announced the winner on the loud speaker as we approached the halfway mark. I hadn't expected to win but was hoping to at least finish before the guy who won got back to Kenya. I was just about to recover psychologically when the second shoe dropped. They announced the women's winner. I don't consider myself a chauvinist, but at that moment I wanted to send all the females on earth back to Venus.

I struggled on to what they call the wall, which is the 19-mile mark. I always thought the wall was a mental thing. I could not have been more wrong. The wall in this case was a serious, and I mean serious, hospital tent. There were doctors, nurses, orderlies, ambulances, priests, rabbis, faith healers and helicopters. I even thought I saw a hearse. I thought to myself, so this is where they filmed the depot field hospital scene from Gone with the Wind and every season of Mash. Miraculously, I pressed forward. I survived a gang of fools who were still lining the street and thought they were helping by yelling, "Only seven more miles!"

Finally, we entered Central Park, which had obviously been enlarged since the last time I was there, now seemingly the size of Wyoming. For the first time since the women's winner, I thought I might finish and then the whole back-to-Venus thing returned to haunt me forever.

A lady came by me wearing a sweatshirt that exclaimed, "Your doors have just been blown off by a 71-year-old woman."

I surrendered and walked in.

When I arrived at the finish line, there was fastidious Pat still polishing, still patting. The rest of the crew was there, too, including my wife, and impressively they had procured a cooler and some beer. On the way to the hotel I developed terminal leg cramps, meaning if I couldn't get relief I was going to die. I tried every way I could to straighten out, but all I accomplished was the total destruction of the beer cooler – ice – beer – water and all – kicked everywhere. Pat, hearing the crunch of styrofoam, realized what had happened, and immediately stopped in the middle of the street intent on one objective – rescuing his floor board. I performed some type of magic show act by levitating and extricating myself from the limo out into the street. Still terminal.

Who comes to my rescue but Ron.

His first move was to put his hands on my chest. I told him I didn't need CPR, I had leg cramps. He told me to be calm. I told him it was hard to be calm with all the pain. He said to be still. I told him to get your hands off my chest you idiot and rub my legs. He said shut up. I said what? He said we've drawn a crowd. I said what do I care? This is New York and there's always a crowd. He said I can't let them see the Juice Plus+® logo on your shirt.

Sandra and I proudly wore our Juice Plus+® shirts in 30 more marathons before the protective specter of Ron Watkins appeared again.

This time, it wasn't leg cramps or the cracking of styrofoam that did us in, it was the click of a camera catching us crossing the finish line in New York – just behind two guys who ran 26 miles in a cow suit.

One cow suit, two guys.

We vowed we would never subject ourselves and our company to that humiliation again. We are officially out to pasture.

Bella

"The whole house lit up like a CSI murder scene."

Almost all who saw the movie The Godfather remember the famous line, "I'll make him an offer he can't refuse." Fewer remember Michael Corleone's answer to his wife's question at the end regarding whether or not he had killed his brother-in-law. The answer was, "No."

One of my dearest friends, Gaspare DiCarlo – who is actually Sicilian born near the town of Corleone – was faced with a somewhat similar situation and decided to give a similar answer to the question of whether or not he had killed the family cat, Bella.

The story began when Bella, who had been a family member for several years, began peeing in the house, pretty much everywhere, including on the furniture. My friend is a hygiene freak. The fact that a cat was peeing where he sat practically drove him up the walls – my friend that is, not the cat.

His first attempt at doing something was to ask his wife to put the cat outside. She refused, citing the fact that the cat had been de-clawed and was, therefore, defenseless. In spite of the smell, she didn't believe the problem was that bad and bought some kind of cat pee detection light to prove it. This move backfired big time when the indicator light came on as they checked their own bed. The whole house lit up like a CSI murder scene.

At this point Bella had used up her eighth life, but my friend

Gaspare was the only one who knew it at the time.

Gaspare tried to be humane about the whole thing. He actually went to a pet psychologist, who explained to him that Bella had become territorial, and the only answer to changing her behavior was to change her surroundings. Exiling her to the basement seemed the only logical move. This lasted only a couple of days when the pee light spotlighted the family pool table.

Heated arguments ensued, but this time it was the woman of the house, supported by all the kids, who said, "No."

Signor DiCarlo was left with one option. "I have to killa my cat and make it looka lika an accidente." His first move was a visit to a pet funeral home, where he was given three options.

Deluxe. This included cremation, service, complete with a priest, and burial, which involved the ashes being scattered in the Poconos – Price $850.

Standard. Cremation, service, and burial in the funeral home cemetery – Price $400.

Economy. Mass cremation – mass burial – Price $200.

After determining that mass did not mean a Catholic service, he chose number three. His only problem, besides catching his cat without anybody knowing about it, was that this "mass" was held only twice per month.

He came up with a plan to get his wife out of the house on the big day, successfully captured Bella, put her in a box in his trunk, and got behind the wheel. Then guilt struck. Not guilt about what he was doing, but how he was doing it. He was afraid that Bella might suffocate in the box, so he opened the trunk and cut air holes in the box. When he arrived at the pet funeral home, he opened the trunk and went inside to make arrangements.

When he returned, Bella was gone. Guilt was replaced by relief. Bella was gone, he had saved $200, and he would not have to face a murder charge. It was time to celebrate so he stopped by his favorite bar, toasted Bella, went to dinner, and stumbled home. His welcoming committee included, guess who?

Bella.

Two weeks later he was able to execute almost the identical plan, except this time, Bella was placed in a cardboard vault.

That night the questions came.

"Did you kill Bella?"

"I can't believe you killed Bella?"

"Daddy, tell us that you didn't kill Bella?"

Taking a page from Michael Corleone himself, my good, honest friend, good husband and father, looked his wife and family in the eye and said, "I can't believe you ask me thata question. NO!!!"

A week later he returned home to a room full of tears, the likes of which he had never seen. It seems a sympathy card from the funeral home had just arrived. Still true to his upbringing, amid this onslaught of contempt, he was able to offer an explanation.

"See I tolda you. I don'ta killa Bella. They did."

Bella never returned to the aforementioned bed, and Gaspare almost never made it back there himself.

Lock Me Up And Throw Away The Key

"It was J.W.'s wife warning them that J.W. was headed to town,
'with his gun fixin' to kill both y'all.'"

My wife's uncle, Myrl, used to be a deputy sheriff in a small Mississippi town where everybody knew everybody and everybody's business.

One Saturday night, he walked into the sheriff's office/combination jail, and noticed that a friend of his and the sheriff's was behind bars. "What'd J.W. do?" he asked.

"Drunk again," answered the sheriff.

From Myrl, "Why didn't you just take him home?"

From the sheriff, "Didn't have nobody to drive his car, and besides I'm tired of him being up here drunk every Saturday night."

"I'll drive his car," Myrl offered, "you can follow me."

"Alright," said the sheriff reluctantly, "Get the damn keys."

So the sheriff drove J.W. home, and Myrl followed in J.W.'s car. When they got to J.W.'s house the sheriff gave him a stern warning about not showing back up in town drunk, or his ass was going to spend the night in the slammer – no questions asked.

A few minutes after Myrl and the sheriff got back to the office the phone rang. It was J.W.'s wife warning them that J.W. was headed to town, "with his gun fixin' to kill both y'all."

"Why does he want to kill us?" Myrl asked.

"For bringing him home to face me," was the answer.

Well, J.W. got there, got disarmed, and got a cot for the night in jail, as promised, with no questions asked.

The next morning Myrl walks into the office to find the sheriff busy with some paperwork. "What you doing?" Myrl inquired.

"Charging J.W.," said the sheriff.

"Hell, that's more trouble than it's worth," Myrl argued. "Let's turn him loose. He's got to be sober by now."

"Alright," said the sheriff, "but if I have to go through this again I'm throwing the damn book at him, and I mean it."

That afternoon they get another call from J.W.'s wife. "He's drunk again. Headed to town again. Gonna kill both y'all again."

"What the hell for this time?" Myrl asked.

"He ain't able to explain to me how come he spent the night in jail and never got charged."

She Was Truly A "Jarrell"

"Her two loves in life were cow manure and crab apples
in any order, and we just happened to live next door
to a pasture full of cows and crab apple trees."

My first dog was called Sparkie. He was named after a kid on a Saturday morning radio show. I don't remember the name of the radio program or too much about Sparkie either. He was an outside mutt and got run over one night after I went to bed. My parents didn't tell me until around noon the next day because they thought I might cry.

They were right.

Then we got a Boston Bulldog puppy we named Buster. He loved people, especially us, but he hated cats – especially the two across the highway – and he hated doghouses – especially the doghouse my father and I built him because it meant he had to stay outside on a lead attached to that doghouse, unable to get inside to us or across the street at the cats.

One day we returned home to find Buster and his doghouse on the porch. He wanted in so badly that he actually pulled his house across the back yard and on to the porch one lunge at a time. From that moment on, Buster became an inside dog, and I never had another dog that didn't live inside. If they were good enough to be my dog they were good enough to live where I did.

We never regretted making Buster a full-fledged member of the household. He never played favorites. He slept with everybody.

He ate what we ate, even vegetables, and aside from the resulting eye-watering gas, he had no shortcomings.

But, sadly, the cats won. One night about dark, he charged across the aforementioned highway in hot pursuit of his archenemies totally oblivious to traffic.

I cried all night and some more the next day. I still miss him.

We had two other Boston's, Commando and Rebel, but they never took the place of Buster. Commando didn't have much personality. Rebel had some health problems including a nervous stomach and habitual halitosis, but he lived long enough to throw up all over my first serious girlfriend when they were introduced.

When Rebel died I wasn't living at home anymore, and I guess I was too old to cry. My parents still waited three months to give me the bad news just in case.

My wife and I decided to get an English Bulldog. Unlike me and Boston Bulldogs, she had a pedigree three feet long – the dog, not my wife. Therefore, she needed at least three names. Since the original owner's name was Long, we decided on Mary Juno Long-Martin. She was an early feminist – my wife, not the dog.

Ms. Mary, Juno that is, was one of nine children, and her owner suspected that she might have been born with some type of stomach problem, since she ate almost as much as her eight brothers and sisters combined. They were all happy to see her go so they could finally get a clear shot at a teat.

We had Ms. Long, Juno that is, checked for every possible dog eating disorder known to veterinary science, but "hearty appetite" was the only thing they could come up with. Godzilla had a hearty appetite; this dog had something beyond that.

Ms. Martin, Juno that is, weighed 64 lbs. on her first birthday. We gave her a cake, which she liked, but Juno would have preferred something else. Actually, two or three of something else. Her two loves in life were cow manure and crab apples – in any order – and we just happened to live next door to a pasture full of cows and crab apple trees. Juno loaded both by the ton, causing bloating the likes of which you've never seen and hope to never see. Once or twice a week we were driving this dog, blown up like a weather balloon, to the vet for a purging process I can't describe to this day without gagging. I'm gagging just a little as I write this. On the positive side, the receptionist at the vet's office fell in love with Juno and didn't live within 10 miles of a crab apple tree or a defecating cow.

Mary Juno Long-Martin soon became Mary Juno Long-Martin-Jones. Life around our house and in our car improved, although I must confess we missed Ms. Long-Martin-Jones – Juno, that is.

One Sunday morning about six weeks after she left, we found her back at our door – in the arms of a wide-eyed Mr. Jones. "This dog is going to eat us out of house and home," was all he had to say. Mary Juno was once again a Martin.

A few weeks and several purges later, a desperation ad we ran was answered by a prominent local physician by the name of Hancock. "Let's see her eat them out of house and home," I gleefully offered, as we drove away from his huge house and through his electronic gate. Less than six months later I heard that Dr. Hancock had sold Juno to a man named Jarrell from Mt. Airy. Evidently, she had eaten a set of Britannica encyclopedias.

Some time later I was in Mt. Airy and saw the name Jarrell on a mailbox. I stopped to inquire if this might be the proud owner of a rather large female English Bulldog with a long line of names, but answering to but one – Juno that is.

"Nope," came the reply, "that's my first cousin."

After following directions that included two tobacco barns, a large oak tree, and a graveyard, I finally arrived at cousin Jarrell's. Sure enough, there was Juno, big as ever, and every bit as glad to see me as the day I introduced her to cows and crab apples. Mr. Jarrell was everything you would expect a dog lover to be. Juno was his "all-time favorite." The kids were "plum crazy" over that dog. She was truly a "Jarrell." We talked on for a piece, and Mr. Jarrell saw me to the car and closed the book on Mary-Juno-Long-Martin-Jones-Martin-Hancock-Jarrell.

"I'll tell you one thing," he said, "that's the eatinist one dog ever I saw."

Know your way ...

41. Always focus on your ultimate objective and think long term first. It doesn't do any good to drive faster if you're headed in the wrong direction, much less if you're headed for a wreck.

42. It's one thing to deal with lack of success – you forgot where you were going. It's another to deal with success – you forget where you came from.

43. Everybody is born with a blackboard. Some people don't get an eraser and badly need one. Quoting Willie Nelson, "Forgetting seems to take the longest time."

44. Don't pre-suffer prematurely.

45. There is no such thing as just the least bit crooked.

Don't Forget Where You Came From

"They had never seen a dog that could even come close to Old Salesman."

Four friends of mine lived to bird hunt and were always dying to tell you about it. Each year they and all their shotguns would go to Alabama, rent a bird dog, and blast away.

This particular year they rented a dog named Old Salesman and paid the premium price upon the advice of the elderly gentleman in charge of dog rentals. "He's worth every penny," said the man.

Sure enough, he was.

They had never seen a dog that could even come close to Old Salesman. All year long they couldn't wait to go back. They called in advance to reserve this special dog, and even though the price had almost doubled, they gladly paid the difference.

Their second year was even more enjoyable, and the third even more than that, in spite of another hefty price increase.

The fourth year was different. When they called to see if Old Salesman was available the answer was, "Sure." They were elated. But when they asked how much the price was, it was lower, much lower, even lower than the first year they rented him.

"Is he injured?" they asked. The answer was, "No". "Is he passed his prime?" The answer was, "Not at all." When they asked why the drop in price the old man told them.

"Well," he said, "Some fellas from Atlanta came over here last spring and got to drinking and forgot his name. They called him Old Sales Manager, and the son-of-a-bitch ain't done nothing since but sit on his ass and bark."

Watch For The Sign Of The Goat

"I was flipping through a facts application on my iPhone and learned that in the average box of corn flakes, there is more nutrition in the box than in the flakes."

As people around the world continue to become more concerned about the quality, the cost, and even the availability of their food source, more and more companies are looking for ways to help them address those concerns.

We recently introduced a product called the Tower Garden, which enables families to grow a wide variety of fruits and vegetables literally on their patio. As we were in the process of introducing the Tower Garden, I couldn't help but think back to a time almost 50 years ago when I should have seen the need for something like that even then.

My roommate and I sold pots and pans during college and lived in a house complete with a yard. Our boss was a guy who liked to dream up wild contests, where, in most cases, the loser was "rewarded" more than the winner. Many times there were teams involved, and in this particular case, we had to keep a goat at our house. We lost the "Get Your Goat" contest.

We picked up the goat in my roommate's Plymouth Valiant. In the trunk. Don't ask or tell the humane society how we got him in the trunk.

When we asked the owner what the goat's name was, he said, "D.A."

"D.A.?" we asked.

"Yes, Dumb Ass."

We brought D.A. home and tied him to a tree in our yard. Apart from the trunk-stuffing episode, we were animal lovers at heart, so we gave D.A. plenty of slack when we tied him to a tree so he could reach some bushes he seemed to be lusting after.

Almost immediately, our new goat backed up to the tree and ran as hard as he could to the far end of the yard and jerked himself completely off the ground. After about six times, my roommate and I both looked at each other and nodded. Now we knew why they called him Dumb Ass.

We were able to wrestle Dumb Ass to the ground and tether him to an outside faucet near the porch. Now the problem was starvation, not a spinal cord injury. We asked a neighbor, who looked like he knew what goats ate. Without hesitation he said "cornmeal and sorghum syrup." Well we were a little short on those items in our pantry, but we did have some corn flakes and maple syrup. We split the box open, sat it near Dumb Ass, and poured the syrup on. Dumb Ass then proceeded to scatter the whole concoction on our porch – flies 'til Christmas – and happily eat the box.

What specifically made me think of D.A. after 50 years?

I was flipping through a facts application on my iPhone and learned that in the average box of corn flakes, there is more nutrition in the box than in the flakes.

Just think, Dumb Ass was decades ahead of his time and should have been named Smart Ass. Sorry about that trunk thing, S.A.

Redneck Revue

"In my travels, I have run across, into, over, and sometimes run with, several distinctly different breeds."

Rednecks aren't all the same. While they all have certain traits in common – rusty pickups, nose picking, lock picking and lottery number picking, for example – the specific neck you'll see depends on your neck of the woods.

In my travels, I have run across, into, over, and sometimes run with, several distinctly different breeds.

In Piedmont, North Carolina, where I come from, you have a white-socks-wearing... car-race-going... third-shift-working... pale-looking... Gastonia textile neck.

Over in east Tennessee and east Kentucky, you have a three-toothed... liquor-making... meth-cooking... sister-jumping... narrow-faced... hollow-eyed... cave-dwelling type neck who would JUST AS SOON kill you as look at you.

In south Georgia, there's the brogan-shoed... tractor-driving... Massey Ferguson cap-wearing... red-faced farming neck. As for north Georgia, well, we all know what happened to Ned Beatty on that river.

Where Arkansas, Mississippi, and Tennessee come together, you have a big-ass-tire-pickup-driving... bass-fishing... deer-hunting... rasslin'-watching... Clinton-hating... Branson-going neck.

In Oklahoma and Texas resides the cheek-and-gum-snuff-packing... chaw-chewing... rodeo-going... cowboy-hat-wearing... bow-legged... square-dancing... long-neck-drinking neck, while in Louisiana and south Mississippi you have a crawfish-head-eating... gator-baiting... coon-hunting... pulp-wooding... Pentecostal neck.

They're plenty of necks up north, too. The upstate New York hibernating... homemade-wine-making... bib-overall-wearing... lapsed-Mennonite neck comes to mind as does an end zone full of Cleveland necks at a Browns game. Then, there's the Western Pennsylvania one-large-size-fits-all... Eastern-European... very friendly and completely clueless neck.

Don't think that California doesn't have rednecks. Just because they've got their own kind of tie-dyed crazy, tend to live in old school buses and smoke grass instead of mowing it, doesn't rule them out at all. Such redneck staples as car racing, bass fishing, bowling, wife beating, TV preachers and ass smells are all alive and well in the Golden state. Just check out the crowd at a Raiders game. From a distance. A considerable distance.

But in south Alabama you have, in my humble opinion, the ultimate, quintessential redneck representative – the pure-bred... extra-large... filling-station-sitting... flat-top-sporting... Pabst Blue Ribbon-drinking, stained-tee-shirt-wearing... ass-crack-showing... tire-tool-wielding... tattooed ex-navy neck who would RATHER kill you than look at you.

If I've offended anyone by leaving out your particular neighborhood neck, I apologize.

I'm sure he's one nasty piece of work.

Past Pocatello

*"Boys, life's going to throw you some curves. If you can't hit 'em…
you'll always be stuck in Pocatello."*

When I reflect on life's lessons, I can't help but remember those learned in sports, especially on the baseball field. My father was a baseball historian of some note, and I owe him a lot for what he taught me about the game.

I learned some things off the field. I even learned some geography – Cleveland was on a lake and a river – Chicago was on a lake and windy, too – St. Louis was on a river, and they made Budweiser there – Pittsburgh was the Iron City, and they made steel there. New York had a subway that ran to Brooklyn and to the Bronx, and that's where Yankee Stadium was – Boston was still cold in April, and San Francisco was even colder in July. I even learned that in Montreal they spoke French, trois strikes and you're out.

I learned some philosophy. Winners never quit – Babe Ruth struck out more times than anybody else – Lou Gehrig played in 2,000 straight games – Mickey Mantle had bad knees, but he never complained. I hated the Yankees, but underneath I had respect. One Yankee, Yogi Berra, taught me "it ain't over 'til it's over." Of course, he also said, "I really didn't say everything I said." I can relate.

I learned that English is not always a prerequisite for success, ironically not from Roberto Clemente or Tony Perez, who spoke

English as a second language, but from Dizzy Dean and Casey Stengel, who spoke something that wasn't English at all.

I learned that Jackie Robinson was not only as good as anybody, but better than most.

I learned that nobody was bigger than the game itself, not even my hero, Pete Rose.

But most of my lessons came with my spikes on. There was no classroom like the diamond.

I learned to watch my coach – not to miss a signal. I learned to run everything out – you never know. I learned to call the other guy off and to let him call me off. I learned that everybody makes errors, even Ryne Sandberg.

I learned to always force the runner back to the base he came from. It's like playing on house money.

I learned that tobacco made you sick. I once swallowed a chew trying to get out of the way and catch a low liner at the same time. Got down for the liner, threw up the chew.

I learned that every bounce wasn't fair and that umpires weren't always right, but it didn't matter – they had the final say.

I learned to be aggressive, but not too aggressive. A good catcher could throw you out, and a lefthander with a good move could leave you hung out like grandmother's laundry.

I learned the importance of teamwork, but also that one good pitcher and a left-handed power hitter could make a good team great.

I learned to practice, to warm up, to get in front of the ball, and a hundred, a thousand other things. But the most important lesson I ever learned was that there was such a thing as a curve ball. Oh, how I hated to face a side arm throwing lefthander.

I remember my summer league coach, who was also our one-man police force. His name was Burleigh Simmons. What a great name for a baseball player. And Burleigh was a player. The best I had ever seen up close. He could hit – he could run – he had a great glove, and he could throw you out at third base with a frozen rope from right field in a heartbeat.

Burleigh had played in the minors for a few years at various places and had made it all the way to Pocatello, Idaho, but never any further. He was our hero and our friend in sort of a priest-like way. We didn't have a Catholic church in our little town, but we had a confessional booth. It was Burleigh's '57 Chevrolet, which sat discretely parked with Burleigh inside every night looking for out-of-town speeders to help keep us in bats and helmets.

We spent many hours in that old Chevy listening to Harry Carey and the St. Louis Cardinals. Harry became a Cubs man later, but back then he was all Cardinals and so was Burleigh.

Burleigh would fill in rain delays with stories about his travels. We always wondered why he never made it past Pocatello, and one night we got up the nerve to ask.

"Boys," he said, "it's pretty simple. Ole Simmons couldn't hit a curve ball. When you get past Pocatello they figure that out and that's all you ever see."

It was the ultimate lesson. Many was the time he would remind us when things weren't going well. "Boys, life's going to throw you some curves. If you can't hit 'em you'll never play in the big leagues – you'll always be stuck in Pocatello."

I've found life to be no different. The curve ball just has a different name. Instead of "Uncle Charlie" and "Captain Hook," it can be a personal tragedy, an illness, an accident, an addiction. Rather than "Ole Epheus," it's a business gone sour, a company gone broke, a loved one gone. I've always admired those who could hang in there under the worst of conditions. You've just got to wait, be patient and not give ground. And you never go to bat looking for a curve, that's the biggest mistake of all.

Burleigh and I lost touch over the decades. I went to college and moved away. He got a job as a revenue agent up in the mountains. I'm sure old Simmons has seen some sliders and backsliders and some serious foul balls in that capacity.

A couple of years ago I had a chance to go through the town where Burleigh had moved. I had a little time so I decided to pay him a visit. I called but there was no answer. I stopped at a gas station and asked the attendant if he knew Burleigh Simmons.

"Sure," he said, "he lives up on Eagle Mountain, but he's not home." Burleigh's wife had had a stroke and she was partially paralyzed. He had taken her to Duke hospital for treatment. Simmons had seen another curve.

I asked the attendant where I could get a bite to eat. He gave me directions to Miss Mabel's for the best "fried chicken steak in town." I drove to the end of the street, turned left and started looking for Miss Mabel's. It was almost dark. Suddenly light appeared. It was the ball ground across the street. I couldn't help but look, and there was this sign right in front of me. The sign read:

THIS FIELD IS NAMED FOR JAMES BURLEIGH SIMMONS – FOR HIS MANY YEARS OF SERVICE TO THE LITTLE LEAGUE OF THIS COMMUNITY.

Burleigh made it past Pocatello, a long way past.

A Principal's Principles

*"At first, my father decided to just respond to
the Reverend with one word, 'Great.'"*

After my father retired from his job as a school principal, he was asked to run for the North Carolina State House of Representatives. Considering his political views and those of the electorate that would decide his fate, it would have taken a miracle for him to have won. It did, and he won.

The most politically charged issue of his first term was the equal rights amendment giving women equal status to men in the work place. Ironically, a large segment of the faith community in our area was opposed to this amendment.

Here is a sample of a letter my father received during his time in office. The names have been changed to protect the "blessed":

> Dear Principle [sic] Martin,
>
> I want you to know that my entire congregation is against equal rights for women. If this passes it will just be a question of time until we will be voting on women deacons and even pastors. If you vote for this you will not only be punished on election day but will have to answer for it on judgment day as well.
>
> Respectfully,
> Pastor John Renegar
> Shiloh Baptist Church

At first, my father decided to just respond to the Reverend with one word, "Great." After some thought, he wrote Pastor Renegar the following letter:

Dear Brother Renegar,

It is always good to hear from people with opposing views, because it gives me a chance to explain my position to them.

While I personally would be in favor of women being deacons and pastors, this proposed amendment makes no reference to religion at all.

In addition, if your reasoning is correct, would not the failure of this amendment have an adverse effect on your church and mine as well? In our case we might have to get rid of our choir director and our pianist, our Sunday school might have to close, and vacation Bible school would certainly be canceled.

In spite of the fact that you and I differ on this amendment, I would assume both of us believe in the first amendment. In that amendment's spirit, I will be glad to read your letter to the entire North Carolina House of Representatives, on the condition that you read mine to your entire congregation.

Sincerely,
Principal Martin

Beware of people who know they're right. Especially beware of people who speak for God.

Personally yours ...

46. Pay for everything you use personally including stamps (see Harry Truman). Don't accept gifts from suppliers that you can't eat or drink.

47. It is possible to do well and good. Human should be spelled with an 'e' on the end.

48. It's not what you know. It's not what you do with what you know. It's what you do with what you don't know.

49. When you dwell, dwell on the future and not the past. "The true meaning of life is to plant trees, under whose shade you do not expect to sit." – Nelson Henderson

And finally ...

50. All that matters is how the people who really know you feel about you.

Newton Rules

"It didn't matter if there were two people or 22 at our house, he knew exactly where the geometric center of activity was and always perfectly positioned himself there."

Sir Isaac Newton's Laws of Physics forever changed how we thought about the world we lived in, not to mention apples. Sandra and I decided to name our first dog in his honor, since taking on that responsibility with our busy schedule might change our lives forever as well. Turns out, he became the apple of our eye.

Newton entered our lives at age eight by way of being rescued and lived to the ripe old doggy age of 16. While the two Newtons never met, there was a remarkable resemblance between the two, both physically and mentally.

Our Newton understood geometry.

It didn't matter if there were two people or 22 at our house, he knew exactly where the geometric center of activity was and always perfectly positioned himself there. He was always in the middle of everything. On occasion he ate at the table with the manners of an English Earl. He went on every family vacation, swam and rafted in our pool, and house guests would more than likely find him in the bed with them come morning. He wore a tuxedo on New Year's Eve and actually passed out once from too much champagne. Don't start with me. Everybody gets champagne at our house on New Year's Eve.

I have often referred to Newton during speaking engagements when I'm trying to emphasize initiative and involvement:

> Newton was always in the middle of things; you need to be in the middle of things. You can't win a game from the sidelines or as a spectator in the stands or on the couch. You can't let others take control of your destiny. Whatever the situation, whatever the issue, whatever the circumstances, get in the middle of it. Just like Newton.

Newton also understood physics, certainly that part about a force being met with an equal force.

He knew if he loved us we would love him back. He knew if he loved others they would love him back. He even loved our cat, and she loved him back. They ate from the same bowl, when he was not eating at the table, of course. Everybody knows that cats don't eat at the table.

Newton was famous in a quiet way. He never wrote a book or composed a song or showed up on reality TV, but he was known. He seldom left our yard except to go on walks and family vacations, yet his groomer closed for the afternoon when he died; our pool man cried when he heard the news; our garbage man left a sympathy card, and we had to ask our neighbor's kid to help park cars for his funeral.

The eulogy was short and simple.

He was a gift from God, and we would try to follow his example. As long as we lived we would always try to stay in the middle of things that mattered just like he had always done, and we would try our best to love everybody just like he did.

Reminding us to apply Newton's Laws was his legacy. We hope it will be ours as well.

Tribute To One Of My Boys

*"On the other hand, had we taken a vote for the most popular kid
we would have needed only one ballot."*

I first met Clay Robertson when I was trying to put together
a neighborhood basketball team. I was looking, in basketball
vernacular, for a "space eater," and Beverly told me Clay might
just fit the bill. She failed to mention speed, and I took Clay sight
unseen.

We wound up with a tennis player, a swimmer, a soccer player
who went on to kick field goals for LSU, one basketball player, and
a tight end. Robbie Witt was our center, and Clay, well, Clay was
our "trailer."

We won 30 games and beat everybody we played. We had
three rules – listen, hustle and don't be selfish. They were the most
unselfish group of kids I have ever been around. If we had taken
a vote for most valuable player, we would have had three or four
candidates and probably gone through at least that many ballots
to name a winner.

On the other hand, had we taken a vote for the most popular
kid we would have needed only one ballot. The results would
have been unanimous, and the winner would have been Clay.

From the size of the crowd here today, I'm certain if a poll had
been taken at CBHS or at the Pike House at Ole Miss or on Millers
Farm the results would have been the same.

Beverly, Clay was one good kid.

When something this bad happens to a good kid like Clay we all ask God the same question. Why is life so unfair? God actually answered that question once, except it wasn't really God, it was George Burns in the movie "Oh God."

A little girl asked God, played by George Burns, why is life so unfair? Why do some people seemingly have everything and others nothing? Why are some condemned to a life of sickness and pain and others not?

George Burns answered this way. "Well, when I made this world I thought I did a pretty good job. I got lots of compliments, and I even gave myself a day off. But, you know, there were some things I couldn't do, some things even I couldn't figure out. I couldn't make a top without a bottom. I couldn't make a front without a back, nor an up without a down. I could not bring someone joy without sorrow. I just couldn't figure it out."

Well, if God couldn't figure it out, how are we to?

But maybe the real God has figured it out after all. Maybe he's made a place with no bottom and no down. Maybe there is a place with only joy and no sorrow. Our faith and our hope tell us there is, and that same faith and hope tell us that, Clay, this good kid, is in that place.

Flush With Confidence

"Get a $100 bill and put it in your pocket."

When I first got into sales I couldn't sell. I knew everything there was to know (which is different from needed to know) about the product. I could raise and overcome objections and walk and chew gum all at the same time. But I couldn't close a screen door.

Bordering on desperation, I asked my sales manager what was wrong.

"It's pretty simple," he answered. "You're broke and you think everybody else is broke."

Wow, great, terrific. Eureka, what a revelation. I'm broke because I can't sell, and I can't sell because I'm broke. Chicken and egg tail chaser.

I didn't even have another question, much less an answer.

Luckily he did.

"I tell you what you do. Get a $100 bill and put it in your pocket. Take it everywhere you go; sleep with the damn thing. You'll be surprised what it'll do for your image, your attitude, and your closing rate."

The currency of confidence.

Sometimes being green and gullible is a blessing, and I've been carrying green ever since. I followed his advice and until this day, I will not be caught dead – yes, I will take it with me –

without a serious amount of cash in my pocket.

Even when I run, I'm flush. I call it my mugger's insurance. If I am ever accosted, my wad will travel a long way toward getting my ass out of sight before they stop counting.

I'm confident about that.

I'm Trying To Get To Heaven Before They Close The Door

"The original Forrest Gump passed away and found himself standing in front of the Pearly Gates. Since no one seemed to be there, he knocked."

I guess my thoughts about religion might be summed up in one sentence. Faith and certainty are by definition two very different things.

I believe no two people on earth share the same understanding when it comes to spiritual matters. The best example of how well-meaning people can reach totally different conclusions regarding the same thing is the story of Forrest Gump.

The original Forrest Gump passed away and found himself standing in front of the Pearly Gates. Since no one seemed to be there, he knocked.

"Is anyone home?" asked Forrest.

"Yes," answered St. Peter.

"May I come in?"

"Only when you answer some questions," St. Peter replied.

"What are the questions?"

"Question one is how many days in the week start with a T?"

"That's easy," said Forrest, "two - today and tomorrow."

St. Peter was amused at the answer, gave Forrest a checkmark and continued, "Question two is how many days are there in May?"

"Easy again," said Forrest. "There are seven – Sunday, Monday, Tuesday, Wednesday, Thursday, Friday and Saturday."

Once again, and a bit bewildered, St. Peter checked the box. "Okay," he said, "This one is tricky. What is God's first name?"

"Tricky?" answered Forrest. "That's the easiest one yet! It's Andy."

"Andy?" St. Peter asked. "Where in the world did you hear that?"

"In church," said Forrest. "It's in the hymnbook. Andy walks with me, Andy talks with me, Andy tells me I am his own."

"Enter, son."

My father was a liberal Baptist, an apparent contradiction but may just about cover the entire religious spectrum. He left me lots of words of wisdom. Some I remember well were:

Don't cheat at Solitaire.

Jesus was the most inclusive person who ever lived.

I can't understand why so many so-called religious folks are afraid of knowledge.

Works strengthens faith; they are inseparable.

When Martin Luther King was teaching theology at Morehouse College, he assigned his students the task of defining true service. The following poem by William Blake was on his desk the next morning:

> I sought my soul,
> But my soul I could not see.
> I sought my God,
> But my God eluded me.
> I sought my friend,
> And I found all three.

If I could say a prayer for myself, and everybody else, it would probably be this:

God, you are infinite. Don't let our religion make you finite.

God, you are omniscient. Don't let us be afraid of knowledge.
God, you are omnipresent. Don't let us search for you only in a church.
God, you are omnipotent. Don't let us think we can do without you.

Can I get an Amen?

Title from Bob Dylan's "Trying to Get to Heaven"

Last Impressions

"Long after pastor John had been figuratively and almost literally tarred and feathered, which wasn't long, I remembered her words."

One Sunday, the new preacher came to our house for dinner.

My mother invited a couple of neighbors and prepared her Sunday best, which was a roast, green beans, carrots, mashed potatoes, tomatoes from the garden, creamed corn, Waldorf salad, sweet tea, and, of course, lemon pie.

Between bites and stories from my father, pastor John entertained us with stories and, as that type of event goes, this one went well.

After the pastor left there was the usual hour of judgment. For the most part, the comments were favorable. They ranged from, "If he eats like that every day he won't last long," to, "The potatoes got cold during the blessing," to, "He makes a very good first impression, I'll say that."

My mother had a speaking impediment – my father – but when she overcame it and spoke, she expressed herself succinctly and with purpose. "Last impressions are a lot more important than first ones," she said.

Long after pastor John had been figuratively and almost literally tarred and feathered, which wasn't long, I remembered her words.

No truer ones were ever spoken.

About the Author

*"To build a stable and lasting company that will help
as any people as possible realize their dreams"*

Those are the words that motivated Jay Martin when he founded NSA in 1970, the words that motivate him today as President and CEO, and the words of the company's mission statement cast in bronze at the front door of the headquarters in Collierville, Tennessee.

Jay Martin is a man of his words.